Critical Path
Hiring

Critical Path Hiring

*How to Employ
Top-Flight Managers*

Philip R. Matheny
The Matheny Consulting Group

Lexington Books

D.C. Heath and Company/Lexington, Massachusetts/Toronto

94843

Library of Congress Cataloging-in-Publication Data

Matheny, Philip R.
Critical path hiring.

Includes index.
1. Executives—Recruiting. I. Title.
HD38.2.M37   1986   658.4′ 07111   85-45472
ISBN 0-669-11789-7 (alk. paper)

Published simultaneously in Canada
Printed in the United States of America
Casebound International Standard Book Number: 0-669-11789-7
Library of Congress Catalog Card Number: 85-45472

The paper used in this publication meets the minimum requirements of
American National Standard for Information Sciences—Permanence
of Paper for Printed Library Materials, ANSI Z39.48-1984.
⊗TM

ISBN 0-669-11789-7

The last numbers on the right below
indicate the number and date of printing.

10 9 8 7 6 5 4 3 2 1

95 94 93 92 91 90 89 88 87 86

to Jeanette

Contents

Foreword

George S. Odiorne

Afer more than 100 years of trying to be scientific in management, most managers and employers really do a terrible job of
hiring people. When Frederick Taylor, the "Father of Scientific
Management," first expounded his four-part theory of Scientific
Management in 1895, the second of these four principles called
soberly for the "selection and development of workmen" as one of
the four keys to his system. It swept industry as the savior of companies. In 1904, Hugo Munsterberg of Harvard proposed that psychological testing would help employers pick people more scien-
tifically than old fashioned intuitive methods. In World War I, in
1917, a revolutionary committee on classification of personnel in
the Army used tests to pick and assign people to suitable military
jobs. Thus, it's plain that people have been wrestling with the problem of how to hire the right people for the right job for many
decades. What has been the result?

Not all that hot, really. During the seventies and eighties, over
two dozen large corporations running billions of dollars hired new
presidents only to fire them within a year or two. International
Harvester, AM International, Puritan Industries, RCA, NBC, Wickes
Corporation, Coca-Cola, ITT, and dozens of others churned top
people after conducting lengthy and painful searches to find a
messiah as their corporate leader.

Charlie Revson, the founder of the fabled Revlon empire,
churned vice presidents like Kleenex. A. Robert Abboud, as chairman of First National Bank of Chicago, was reported to have "caused
more than 200 executives to quit" during his eight years at the top
of that institution. When he was finally dropped over the side by his

board, he joined Occidental Petroleum under Dr. Armand Hammer, the crusty owner of that giant energy firm, only to meet the same fate himself—hired then fired. Clearly, there is still some room for improvement in the way we hire people for responsible positions. Usually, at the peak levels of the billion dollar organizations, the losers don't get hurt financially for they have a sufficiently dim view of the hiring process that they lock their new employers into fat contracts which reward them with high six-figure termination deals in the event they are thrown overboard. All of this, of course, merely touches the tip of a giant iceberg when it comes to bad hiring. Down in the ranks where there is no nosy reporter to probe into the slaughter of people who were poorly chosen, the turnover is equally high. We simply don't know how to hire people to fit the jobs, and Taylor's dictum is still worth shooting for. At the same time, it gets no easier but harder to hire well.

Laws and government regulations have risen in an amazing web of complexity to govern the hiring process in the past decade. Larger and larger numbers of people fall into protected categories, including racial groups, ethnic minorities, women, old people, the handicapped, veterans, and a few other categories of people who are surrounded by constraints on their hiring and firing.

That's why Phil Matheny's book is a real contribution to an important problem. His system for hiring the right person for the right job has two tremendous virtues: (1) *It is systematic.* The idea of Critical Path Hiring, in plain talk, means that you start by defining where you want to go in your hiring before you start recruiting and screening. This is the beginning. Having started at the right beginning you then proceed from one step to the next and then to the next in proper order until you get where you want to be. Don't be fooled by his references to science, for it's also laden with another important value. (2) *It makes sense.* One of the most uncommon ingredients in most hiring practice is the element of common sense, which is grounded in experience. Phil has such experience for he has made a fine career and an enviable reputation in hiring people and helping others to hire good people. He has crystalized his many years of experience in this fine book. It doesn't offer you any magic bullets which will assure that you'll hit the right person without sweating out the details. You don't have to use palmistry, graphology, phrenology, stress tests, or brain waves. It doesn't involve the worst of all possible systems—letting a committee decide—as done in hiring college administrators (which accounts for the management troubles in most colleges). It says that you figure out where you want to be after the person gets on the job, and backtrack from there to the beginning. You then follow a critical path to your goal. Nobody yet has developed a wart-free method of hiring people with a perfect track record, but Phil Matheny's book can improve your statistical batting average enough to make it pay off handsomely if you study it, follow it, try it, and work at it.

St. Petersburg, Florida, 1985

Preface

Top-flight executives—those who are exceptional performers—have always been in short supply. They are energetic, dedicated and highly skilled professionals who work within a disciplined, ethical framework. They are "team" players—teachers and mentors—who lead, develop and motivate their people. They are the reason some businesses succeed grandly, and others—sometimes even those with better products and services—succeed only modestly or not at all.

Business leaders and government officials who seem to consistently pick winners and surround themselves with highly competent and dedicated managers do not possess an innate ability to recognize management talent. They have simply acquired a skill. Taken as a group, they are careful observers who follow a methodology of executive selection that they have evolved and refined through experience. It works for them and they do not allow themselves to be dissuaded from it—by either pressure or emotion. They will not accept average performers.

Little has been written on the logic by which those skilled in management selection carry on the hiring process. This is unfortunate because the long-run cost of selecting the wrong person for a responsible management position is frightening. Just as good management is a critical ingredient in the success of a company, poor management will assure poor performance or failure.

This book describes a methodology and procedure for management selection which, if assiduously applied, will save you from most, if not all, of the common errors that people make in hiring executives. You can also avoid most of the uncommon errors and enjoy a very high level of confidence that you have chosen the best person. It is a proven system, but not a perfect one. Hiring is judgmental and can never be reduced to a science. The saving grace is that if you *do* make a mistake with this process, you will know where and how it happened. That is the foundation of knowledge.

Acknowledgments

The methodology, procedure, and philosophy of Critical Path Hiring has evolved over many years of business experience. It would be appropriate for that reason to recognize everyone who has contributed to and influenced my thinking on management processes and management selection. But that is obviously an impossible task. The decision to write a book on management selection, however, is easier to pinpoint. Various parts of the process first appeared in articles published in the Ohio Manufacturers Association *Newsletter* and other publications in 1981 and 1982. The impetus to incorporate these writings into a book was provided by Newton Brokaw, then executive director of the Industrial Association of Central Ohio, at a breakfast meeting early in 1983. His urging me to do it was the triggering event.

The naivete of would-be authors must be wondrous to behold. They go about writing as though they knew what they were doing. In the process of writing something totally unacceptable the first time around, they get themselves thoroughly hooked on the psychic rewards of communicating via the written word. Such was the case with this book.

Many friends and business associates, too numerous to list in this space, provided valuable insights, suggestions, and, most importantly, encouragement and support for my first efforts at writing this book. The turning point came when Robert C. Albright, Vice President–Training and Development, The Huntington National Bank, Columbus, Ohio, introduced me to George S. Odiorne (Holder Professor of Management at Eckerd College in St. Petersburg, Florida). Dr. Odiorne's advice on how to restructure and rewrite the book for publishing, and his counsel and encouragement throughout the project, would be difficult to overvalue. His willingness to help a fledgling writer was pivotal.

For most of the second effort of writing this book, William A. Kistner of Kistner & Associates, Columbus, and Christopher G. Daflucas, Ph.D., of Midwest Human Resource Systems, Columbus, have served as critics, editors, and ardent supporters. Their assistance is gratefully acknowledged. The manuscript typing and retyping ad infinitum, ad nauseum is the work of Dana Bland and Rae Kirkbride of Administrative Resources, Inc., Columbus. They have kept me grammatically correct.

The permission of *Forbes Magazine* in allowing me to include "The Ten Commandments of Contracts" and the cooperation of Ponderosa, Inc. and Nationwide Insurance Co. in permitting the inclusion of their corporate operating philosophies is deeply appreciated.

Lastly, the thoughtful, knowledgeable, and highly professional editing and packaging of *Critical Path Hiring* by Bruce Katz and his associates at Lexington Books deserve praise and thanks.

Introduction

This is a book about how to avoid $100,000 to $250,000, or even $1,000,000, errors in management selection. It describes in detail the process of identification, evaluation, and selection, and in this sense, it is a classic how-to book. Whether you promote from within or bring in new talent from outside, the people you select to manage your business activities will make the difference between success and profitability on the one hand and mediocrity and marginal operations, perhaps even failure, on the other.

The executives of a business organization are assets (or liabilities) and, like other assets, have to be acquired. They do not normally fall into your lap, like manna from heaven. It is a fact that many managers today who are employed from outside the company enter into their jobs without a clear understanding of: (1) what they will be expected to do in the job; (2) the operating philosophy, attitudes, and values of their new employer; or (3) sometimes even an accurate statement of the basis on which a bonus will be paid. To hire an executive in this way is careless management. If you want an outstanding manager you should be in a position to tell him what you think outstanding management is, in specific terms, and what you are willing to pay for a superior performance. You should also be able to tell an outsider what your corporate operating philosophy is, and the attitudes and values by which the company is run. The first part of this book deals with these issues. If you want to employ outstanding executives, you will first have to sell them on your company, your goals and objectives, and your vision of the future.

When you've done this, you can become a buyer. A smart buyer knows exactly what he is getting in the transaction. The middle chapters tell you how to evaluate, recognize, and select exceptional performers. Follow the Critical Path and there won't be any rude, expensive, and embarrassing surprises down the road.

The remainder of the book tells you how to hang on to good executives once you have them. Outstanding executives will forever be in high demand, and can't be taken for granted. Ignore them, and someone will take them away from you. Count on it.

A critical evaluation of a management candidate's skills, abilities, education and training, and his or her knowledge and experience will give you good insight into whether the person can do the job for which he is being considered. But people often do not perform up to expectation, even though they are well qualified. Just because a person can do the job is no assurance that he will.

There are nine critical qualities—let's call them success factors—which must be considered in evaluating a management candidate if you want to make an accurate prediction of how successful he/she will be in the job. These are: energy level, goal orientation, income expectation, non-monetary work expectations, general ability (i.e., communications skills, arithmetic and logical ability and intelligence), people skills, adaptability and flexibility, and lastly, strength of self-image, and management style.

If you identified all of the people in the work force who would like to be managers, and if you scored each of these people on a scale of 0 to 10 on each of these nine factors, and if you aggregated each person's score (obviously each would score between 0 and 90) and plotted the scores, you would end up with a standard distribution curve something like that shown in figure P–1. The significant thing about this distribution is that the presence or absence of these nine qualities in a person is the reason why some managers are happy, productive and successful while others are unhappy, less productive, and prone to change jobs. Some management positions do not require high intelligence, for example (most of us are average, let's face it), or super energy, or strong monetary motivation. On the other hand, you might think twice about selecting a vice president of sales who did not have strong people skills and a positive self-image.

Generally, the higher the individual's aggregate score (the further along that person is on the curve), the better are the chances of

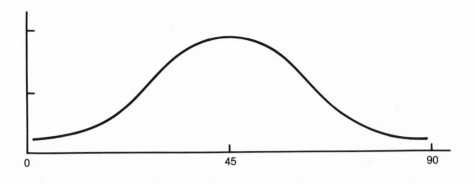

0   45   90

Figure P–1. *Success Factor Distribution Curve*

that person being successful in a management position. Of course, other factors such as education, work experience, and industry knowledge must be considered, but individuals could meet all of these requirements and *still* not be very successful if they lacked strength in the nine personal qualities mentioned above. To select managers with a high potential for success, you have to discipline yourself to look at *all* the factors in the hiring equation. And you have to look at them in the context of the job you are seeking to fill.

Lastly, you have to consider the personal chemistry with the candidate. Unfortunately, even someone rating very high on our scale might not have a pleasing personality. In the final analysis, however, it is better to select a winner who does not play golf on Saturday morning than a charming but only average performer. It's hard to fire a friend you play golf with.

This book describes a discipline and procedure which will bring you a considerable amount of expertise at something you do only occasionally—hiring (or promoting) a manager. It is called Critical Path Hiring and, if you follow it, you will force yourself, in the hiring process, to look at the reasons people really succeed or fail in management. Following the Critical Path will help you do a better job of management selection and you will develop a more successful and profitable company.

In the long run, Critical Path Hiring does not really take more time than other hiring methods. For one thing, you only have to do it once for any one position. The person you select will be right the first time. And you won't find yourself wasting time in the decision process with people who clearly are not suitable. Many people put off the hiring of managers until the situation reaches crisis proportions. Then they hire under pressure without a clear definition of the job to be done. If you hire without careful preparation, you may be hiring executives the way you select your friends. When you choose a friend you logically try to find someone with whom you share common interests and activities—who has a pleasant personality and easy disposition—a good conversationalist on an intellectual level with yourself—someone with whom you are relaxed and comfortable.

This is, however, a very risky way to hire a manager. Notwithstanding, most books on how to find a management position stress the importance of establishing at all costs a comfort level with the hiring executive. There is good reason for this strategy. Many hiring decisions, even at senior management levels, place an inordinate amount of importance on the personal comfort level between the hiring executive and the candidate. Sometimes the interview process never even gets around to the hard issues surrounding the job. If you haven't done your homework in defining what the manager is supposed to do in the job, how can you discuss it intelligently? The pivotal consideration should be whether the individual can succeed in the position.

Notice we did not say "fail" in the position. Statistically speaking, the next person who walks through your door will fall at the midpoint on the previously mentioned distribution curve. If you hire that person, odds are you will get someone who will neither fail resoundingly nor succeed grandly. In short, an average performer.

If you cannot afford to take the time to hire carefully and if you can tolerate "average" performers in your business, this book will not be of much use to you. On the other hand, if you want to surround yourself with winners, *Critical Path Hiring* can help.

Critical Path
Hiring

———

1
Applying the Critical Path
Method to Management Selection

It is nine o'clock on Friday morning. You are sitting at your desk, and across from you is a candidate for a key management position with your company. At least you hope he or she is a candidate. You are about to embark on one of the more difficult tasks that you, as an executive, have to perform—the evaluation and selection of management personnel.

Whether you are the manager of a large company (or a division or department of that company) or the owner of a small one, you have the responsibility to bring into the company people with the management skills needed to further its objectives. If you make a good choice, the individual will quickly become an important contributor. The people in your organization will be happy, motivated, and maybe even inspired by their new leader. You will have strengthened your management team with a new player who shares your commitment to the goals of the company, and who works both hard and effectively. Your life will become a little easier.

If you make a bad choice, something less than this will happen. How much less depends on how bad your choice is. It may be only a little wrong, in which case the new manager is "okay," but not exactly what you had hoped for—not as good a communicator; not as dedicated; not as reliable; not as knowledgeable, imaginative, or responsive; not as people-sensitive. If the choice is really wrong, it is a disaster and can be expensive, divisive, and, to say the least, embarrassing. It could cost you good people, customers, resources, and valuable time.

The Cost of Hiring the Wrong Person

What do we mean when we say "expensive"? Let's add up the cost of hiring the wrong person.

Assume you need a vice president in the $65,000–$75,000 salary range. He will manage a group of seventy-five people and have budget responsibility for $4.5 million. At that level an executive can have a significant impact on the profitability of your operations. The new person is to replace Harry, who is a nice guy and a good friend, but privately you're glad he chose early retirement. You have a nagging feeling that Harry's operation could be run better.

You ask your human resources manager to run ads in the *Wall Street Journal* and a trade journal, and to use whatever other means are needed to come up with some candidates. You ask your human resources manager, Harry, and one other executive to screen all candidates and show the best two or three to you. You make a choice and, for the sake of this example, it isn't a good one. Let's hope it is a really bad one. If it is, you may find out quickly and nip the problem in the bud. Let's presume that in six months you know it isn't working out. Here's what it has cost to date:

		Best Case	*Worst Case*
1.	Management time to recruit (yours, Harry's, human resources manager's, one other executive's)—a minimum of 100 hours @ $50.00/hour	$ 5,000	$ 15,000
2.	Advertising	5,000	10,000
3.	Miscellaneous recruiting costs—travel, etc.	3,000	8,000
4.	Candidate-relocation costs	10,000	35,000
5.	Salary for six months @ $70,000/year	35,000	35,000
6.	Benefits @ 40 percent of salary	14,000	14,000
7.	Costs of poor management		
	Unhappy and lost people	?	?
	Poor utilization of company resources	?	?
	Bad management decisions	?	?
		$72,000 +	$117,000 +

If you are lucky and know with certainty after six months (about the minimum possible time) that the choice is a bad one, and if you react quickly, you may be able to stop the hemorrhaging at $100,000 to $150,000. (The added cost is to buy yourself out of your arrangement with the individual.)

But most choices are not that obviously bad. It could take two or more years to reach the reluctant conclusion that the new person is not working out. By this time you have given him lots of assistance and every opportunity to prove himself and you have now spent over a quarter of a million dollars in direct cash outlays. Unfortunately, that's not the end of it. These are only the direct costs. The cost of poor management could easily double or triple that amount. There is no way to place a true value on lost time or opportunity, on low morale and lost people, or on poor judgment and its effect. In hiring a senior executive, you could easily be making a million-dollar decision, which is plenty of reason for you to be involved.

A Pivotal Task

Although hiring key people is an important responsibility of any business manager, it is not a task that is performed every day. It may only be done on rare occasions. That doesn't make it less important, only more difficult. It is difficult to develop and maintain expertise in something you seldom do.

This book describes a process which will help you select key people with a high degree of accuracy, reliability, and confidence. The process works—and if you follow it you will avoid the pitfalls and problems just described. Further, if you use it in all hiring you will get better at it with experience. You will develop new confidence in your ability to evaluate and predict the performance of people. This will happen because you will be focusing your attention on why people really succeed or fail in management positions. And you will be sharpening your perceptions and ability to recognize key qualities. You will turn the job interview into a learning experience. You will know what questions to ask of that person across the desk from you, and how to accurately and dispassionately interpret the responses you get.

The hiring method described in the following chapters is called "Critical Path Hiring" (CPH). There are two reasons for the selection of this title. First, there is a definite path which must be followed if a careful, successful management selection is to be made. Get off that path and you run the risk of creating a bigger problem than the one you are trying to solve. Second, elements of the Critical Path Method (CPM) of project management have been employed to bring order and discipline to the process, and to communicate the sequence of tasks in the hiring process and how they relate to each other.

Critical Path Hiring assumes that the candidates for a management position need to know what will be expected of them in the performance of the job in question. They too must make informed choices. To do this they must know, as accurately as possible, what the job and the company are all about and what skills, abilities, education, and experience are required. If they fail to obtain this information, they may find themselves in positions in which they cannot function effectively, and which do not meet their career and personal goals and expectations. The Critical Path Hiring procedure solves these issues by requiring the candidates to note, comprehend, comment on, and send a clear signal to the prospective employer that they understand the job, feel they can do it properly, and have a genuine interest in it.

The Critical Path Method

Let's take a quick look at the Critical Path Method and see what it involves before discussing how it can be adapted to the hiring process. CPM was first used by the E.I. Du Pont de Nemours Company in 1957 to control the cost and time-scheduling of new plant construction. Development of the method is credited to Morgan Walker of Du Pont and James Kelley of Remington Rand–Univac. Other early users were Olin Matheson Chemical Company and Union Carbide Company, which also used CPM to control construction and R&D programs.

At approximately the same time, the U.S. Navy was undertaking the development of the Polaris missile system, and the PERT (Program Evaluation and Review Technique) system was developed to manage and control this program. Functionally, CPM and PERT are almost identical and the two terms are used interchangeably. There are small but significant differences in how time to completion of task is estimated between the two systems, but they are not relevant to this discussion. Both CPM and PERT are mathematically ordered networking systems of planning and scheduling for program management; that is, they seek to identify the interdependencies between the many subtasks which make up a large, complex development project. They both lend themselves to such projects through computer processing, analysis, and control.

Dependencies are usually established when the end product of—or resource utilized in—one task is needed to initiate another task. Costs and completion times for the tasks are estimated and a diagram is drawn relating all tasks. A network results which looks something like that shown in figure 1–1.

In a CPM or PERT network, events (specific accomplishments) are represented by circles, while activities leading to the completion of tasks (events) are represented by arrows between circles. Threading its way through the maze of circles is a path between selected events which absolutely must be completed serially (in sequence) if the project is to be successful. This is the *critical path*. Both CPM and PERT establish this path and both are referred to as *critical path scheduling* systems. The critical path can be established on the basis of least time, least cost, or solely on the basis of task dependencies. Usually, all three come into play. By graphically demonstrating the relationships between tasks, critical path scheduling displays what has to be done and when. It also creates a clear understanding of the overall project and assures that no vital activity will be overlooked in its performance.

Critical Path Hiring

By now you are probably wondering what all of this has to do with hiring a manager. Even if you concede that hiring executives is a difficult

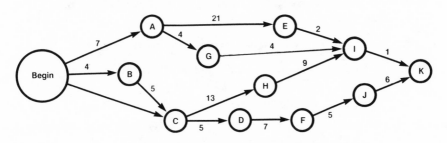

Figure 1–1. *Critical Path Network*

process, it certainly does not compare in complexity with developing an orbiting space station. It just is not that sophisticated a process. Or is it?

Let's examine first what successful executives are like. Entire books have been written on the subject, and there is a risk of oversimplification, but just to name a few qualities: (1) they share your commitment to the goals of the company; (2) they know how to perform their jobs with a minimum of supervision; (3) they are happy, energetic, and motivated by their work; (4) they are team players and people-sensitive; (5) they are efficient, disciplined, and perceptive in carrying out their work; and (6) they are profit-oriented and -motivated. There are many other qualities of course, but these will suffice.

Now let's list some of the considerations which enter into and have impact on the hiring process. How important some of these considerations are will depend on the level of the position you seek to fill within the organization. If you are filling a high-level position from outside the company, they would be critical. If you are filling a lower-level position with the intention of promoting that individual later, they may be less so, but still deserve your attention.

Company-related Considerations

1. Conditions within your industry, and your company's position in the industry

2. The standing of your company vis à vis domestic and international competition

3. Your corporate image and operating philosophy

4. Your company's short- and long-term operating plans and programs

5. The organization and structure of your company

6. World, national, and local economic conditions

Job-related Considerations

1. The level of the position in your organization

2. The duties, responsibilities, and scope of authority which the position carries

3. The peer, upward, and downward interpersonal relationships implicit in the position

4. The skills, abilities, knowledge, and experience that the job requires

5. Your personal preferences

6. The personal preferences of others involved in the hiring decision

Candidate-related Considerations

1. The candidate's career objectives

2. The candidate's perceptions of the industry, the company, and the job

3. The candidate's personality, values, and attitude-forming experiences

4. The candidate's previous work experience

5. The marketplace demand for an individual with the unique qualities of the candidate

6. The candidate's compensation requirements

Each of these eighteen considerations requires some thought and evaluation in the overall task of employing a manager. There are probably others which you thought of as you were reading these. The list could be much longer—and the network of considerations which must be factored into the choice of a manager is, upon reflection, more complex than it appeared to be at first glance.

If a network were drawn up from these considerations alone, it would be quite complex, but our purpose here is not to complicate the hiring process. Rather it is to keep it as simple as possible, consistent with the twin goals of hiring a person who not only can do the job in question, but also will be successful in it once hired.

At this point, you may be thinking, "Yes, but the first twelve of those eighteen considerations are a part of my life as an executive. I live, eat, and sleep them. They condition everything I do every day." That is true. However, you do not hire a manager every day and when you do it is necessary that you discipline yourself to think of these considerations in as objective a way as possible to determine how they impact the hiring decision. The individual you are considering hiring has not been sharing your working environment, some of which will have to be shared if he or she too is to make an informed employment decision. Fortunately, there is a critical path through the hiring process, and for the sake of operating simplicity some of the considerations can be grouped, because they take place at the same time. Figure 1–2 illustrates this Critical Path Hiring network.

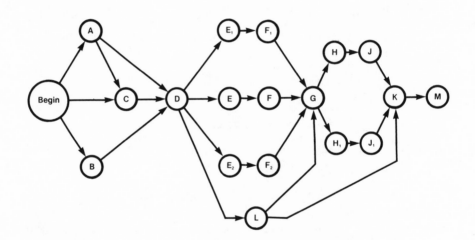

Milestone:

A) Define the position
B) Develop the company presentation
C) Develop candidate sources
D) Initiate the candidate/job analysis process
E) Identify possible candidates
F) Conduct first interview(s)
G) Predict ability of interviewee(s) to perform job

H) Conduct second interview(s) with best candidates
J) Predict ability of interviewee(s) to succeed in job
K) Make hiring decision
L) Check references and background
M) Enter compensation negotiations

Figure 1–2. *Critical Path Hiring Network*

Each of the circles indicated in figure 1–2 represents an event (or "milestone") in Critical Path Hiring. The arrows leading to the milestones represent the activity leading to the completion of the milestone. In normal critical path scheduling, a time would be attached to each of these activities and the sum of these times would be the time to project completion. Time cannot be estimated here for several reasons: (1) milestones E through K will be performed in strict sequence at least once (and possibly more than once, depending on the number of interviewing executives involved in the hiring process) for each candidate; (2) a candidate may be dropped from consideration at any of the milestones; and (3) a number of candidates probably will be considered.

The Critical Path Hiring method is a highly structured system in the sense that certain activities must be performed in reaching each milestone. The milestones cannot be combined or performed out of sequence (except reference checking) without violating the integrity of the method. The balance of this book describes the activities to be performed in reaching each milestone and how to execute each activity. Reaching each milestone yields information essential either to the hiring process or to the evaluation of the candidate, information which feeds and supports the next activity.

What You Can Expect from Critical Path Hiring

If you follow the Critical Path, the following results may be expected:

1. You will have adopted a discipline which is precisely repeatable; a discipline in which you will be able to acquire skill.

2. You will faithfully communicate the vital essential information about the job and the company to each candidate.

3. You will take undue emotion out of hiring and force yourself (and others) to look at what is truly important about the individual in the context of the job.

4. You will have a clearer understanding of what you need to find out in each meeting with a candidate, how to find it out, and when you have obtained the information you need.

5. You will accumulate a file of information on each candidate that can be analyzed and interpreted to help you and others make a more confident hiring decision.

6. You will be able to predict with a high level of confidence the performance of the individual you hire.

How to Do It

A number of years ago, a business machines manufacturer announced a new product, one that appeared to be the long-awaited machine that would open up a whole new market for the company. It was announced with lots of fanfare, promotional literature, and not incidentally, a considerable amount of anticipated performance (throughput) data. The salespeople were told to sell it on the basis of performance and they did. In one case, the applications were developed carefully and when the customer's machine arrived and the system was tested, it was found that it did not operate the way the manual described. It was laboriously slow, so slow, in fact, that it took twelve hours to do six hours of processing. The salesman who sold that machine struggled mightily to make it go faster but to no avail. Finally, he went to his branch manager to work out a compromise acceptable to both the company and the customer. The conversation went something like this:

SALESMAN: Boss, I have tried to make the machine work the way it is supposed to, and it won't. Even headquarters says it won't work quite the way they said it would.
MANAGER: It's your job to make it run successfully. Do it.
SALESMAN: I don't know how to do it.
MANAGER: You want to know how to do it? I'll tell you how to do it. You take off your coat, roll up your sleeves, and you do it. That's how you do it!!!

The salesman was so awed by this bit of "revealed truth" that he simply turned and walked out of the office. When last seen, he was still walking.

Those who witnessed that episode were left with the indelible impression that when you are requesting something that is perceived to be difficult to do, don't stop with the "what to do"; include the "how to do it." The following chapters of this book detail not only the "what" of Critical Path Hiring, but also enough "how" information to enable you to immediately use the method in your hiring activities.

2
Defining the Position
Milestone A

A famous football coach is credited with the observation that when you throw a football up in the air, three things can happen—and two of them are bad. It is, of course, true. It is also both witty and profound. You could say something similar about hiring. At least a half dozen things can happen if you hire someone without a proper position description—and *all* of them are bad.

The Position Definition

The first activity on the critical path is the preparation of a thoughtful, thorough, and concise definition of the position you are seeking to fill. This is the position description—the yardstick by which all candidates will be measured. It can be prepared more or less concurrently with the company or organization definition described in the next chapter, but both of these documents must be substantially complete before beginning the development of candidate sources described in chapter 4.

In Critical Path Hiring the position description is the instrument by which the outsider is introduced to the job. Properly developed, it can convey confidence and a sense of mission to the newly employed manager, allowing him to quickly relate his declared areas of responsibility and authority to the rest of the management organization. It is okay for you to think of this document as a sales brochure for the job, since you would like to have the candidates come to you with a positive attitude about the job and the company.

Defining the position is not a fifteen-minute exercise, and it may, depending on your company, be a real example of participative management in action. Whether you do it independently, by committee, or by task subdivision and assignment, it demands your most careful thought and attention. The position description is your means of communicating specific information to the outsider. If it is obscure, incomplete, or couched in insider's language, it may confuse rather than enlighten. Keep in mind, however, that thoroughness is not merely a matter of piling on more details and more words. As with anything else, there is a point of diminishing returns where position definitions are concerned and there is a danger of being overly detailed. When this happens, key requirements can lose their emphasis. It may also, under these circumstances, telegraph a message to the candidate which is unintentional and undesirable—that the job is restrictive and does not leave room for management resourcefulness and creativity. You certainly do not want that!

Don't Just Take Position Descriptions from the Organization Manual

Your first reaction may be to simply lift the position description out of your company organization manual. This may be a useful point of departure for the preparation of the description, but the odds are one in a million that it would work for you. Here is why:

1. It might not be up-to-date.

2. It might not contain all the needed information expressed in language an outsider can understand.

3. It was not designed for the use to which it will be put in the CPH method.

Hiring a new manager offers an excellent opportunity for thinking through the position from an organizational point of view. Sometimes logical, efficient organization and assignment of responsibilities are lost in trying to accommodate to the strengths or weaknesses of an incumbent manager. Then when that person is replaced, the jury-rigged approach to the position is perpetuated. A word of caution: if you do change the responsibilities of the position, get the changes in place before the new manager gets on board.

Goals of Position Description

A properly prepared position description achieves the following goals:

1. It gives the candidate a positive first impression that the company is purposeful and achievement-oriented.

2. It lets the candidate know what will be expected of him in the job, and what he can expect in exchange for his efforts.

3. It assures that everyone involved in the hiring process is measuring the candidate by the same job parameters.

4. It provides a means of identifying individuals' areas of strength and weakness for their own, as well as their manager's, benefit.

5. It provides a basis for evaluating job performance. It is far from complete in this respect, but it is a start.

6. It is the guide and checklist for conducting the first interview and for preinterview preparation by the candidate. (More on this comes in chapters 4 and 5.)

Writing the Position Description

Remember, you are communicating with someone outside the company. That person may not know the scope and purpose of your business, what place you occupy in the industry, or what challenges and opportunities you face. Do not assume too great a level of awareness of this information. On the other hand, you aren't preparing a disclosure statement, so do not paint a worst-case picture. Rather, strive for a document which fairly and accurately communicates the job requirements and rewards.

The position description should include the following elements:

1. *Job title*

2. *Job overview:* An example of such a statement might be: "Epsilon company is a wholly owned subsidiary of Alpha–Omega, Inc. The position of vice president of finance reports directly to the president of Epsilon and is accountable for the financial control and management of the subsidiary's operating funds. He or she is responsible for the administration of the following activities and functions: data processing; accounting and internal audit; outside accounting firm relations."

3. *Duties and responsibilities:* These are the major or key duties and areas of responsibility. The description of duties should provide enough specific information to indicate not only what is to be done but, ideally, the degree of difficulty involved. (For example, budget review is one function; budget monitoring and control is another.) Insofar as possible the parameters of responsibility and accountability should be spelled out. (For purposes of this discussion, you are *responsible* for the people and functions reporting to you; you are *accountable* to the people above you.) In some position descriptions, so-called "global" statements are used to describe management functions. These statements are usually imbedded in a paragraph of broad general statements of responsibilities associated with the position. These are sometimes quite literate but they do little to nail down specific requirements. An example of a global statement might be: "As vice president of manufacturing, maintain an awareness of trends in factory automation." By contrast, a specific statement would read: "On a quarterly basis, prepare a report for management committee presentation describing cost versus benefit considerations involved in automating a key manufacturing process utilizing state-of-the-art equipment." Some duties may defy such pin pointing, but an effort should be made. Normally this list will include eight to ten duties and responsibilities on which the successful performance of the job will depend. As described in chapters 4 and 5, candidates will be asked to comment in writing on their ability to perform each of these duties. If your description is too general, their responses will also be.

4. *Skills and abilities:* This section of the description should detail the minimum skills, abilities, and industry knowledge required to perform the duties listed.

5. *Training, education, and experience:* Let's face it, every job does not require a Harvard M.B.A. Hiring someone who is overtrained can be as counterproductive as hiring someone who is undereducated. Although it is not easy, and there is a natural tendency these days to say "college degree required," try to analyze what the job really needs and specify the minimum rather than the maximum requirements. If on-the-job experience or specialized training will substitute for formal class work, say so. That way you will not be screening out a potentially valuable employee for arbitrary reasons. Education is only one bargaining chip the potential employee brings to the table. Some people get their B.S. degree at age 50 and an M.B.A. at 52.

6. *Reporting structure:* This section of the job description identifies to whom the position reports; what groups, functions, and departments report to it; and how many managers and other people are involved. Depending on the position, it may also be desirable to indicate where the position fits into the overall structure of the company. This is not to say that a detailed organization chart ought to be included. It may be useful, however, to at least mention peer relationships.

7. *Profit responsibility:* All companies are in business to make a profit, so any management position description should find a place to speak of profit-consciousness. If there is direct return on investment (ROI), budget, or sales responsibility, it should be so stated. As in the case of reporting structure, this is not the place for details, but some indication of profit responsibility is appropriate.

8. *Special requirements:* Management positions very often require extensive travel, entertainment of employees and customers both in and outside the home, active community involvement, and national trade association participation. Some demand the understanding or even the active involvement of

the spouse. In an age of two-career marriages, it is important that these considerations be expressed if they apply. Women are no more likely than men to have constraints on their personal time. Similarly, if hiring an individual requires a change of residence, it is absolutely essential that this be stated so there can be complete agreement on this requirement before the individual is employed.

9. *Compensation:* Of all the information included in a position description, compensation data is the most controversial. You can build a convincing argument for putting it in or leaving it out, depending on your point of view. In most formal salary-administration systems, the salary grade range is fairly wide for management people so there is a good deal of room for negotiating. Still, it is desirable to bring someone in close to the midpoint of the grade, or slightly below it, if possible.

It is a lot easier to hire if money is no object, but most people have to be concerned about internal–external equity (the relationship between salaries paid inside and outside the company for similar positions). One way to try to maintain such equity is to say, "Look, this is the salary range and we are shooting for the midpoint. Do we talk or not?" If you can get at least an approximate understanding on this point up front, you can go on to other matters with some confidence that your time is not being wasted. It also makes negotiating easier later on. You may want to compare your targeted salary range for the position with salary survey information. This data may be obtained from a variety of sources at the national, regional, or local level. In using survey data, be sure that your position definition fairly matches the data being quoted. Comparable position titles are not sufficient to permit an accurate comparison.

Critical Path Hiring is based on objectivity, not emotion. Salary negotiations can be agonizing if there is doubt as to whether candidates are really worth what they are asking. Everything about this method of hiring is designed to increase your confidence in your judgment of this question, which can increase peace of mind where compensation is concerned.

If a bonus based on accomplishing job objectives or other performance parameters is included, it should be described, usually as an anticipated percentage of base salary, along with mode of payment. Stock options, profit sharing, and fringe benefits should be stated also. Sometimes perks are used as bargaining chips in negotiations. Do not mention them unless they are a part of the normal compensation package.

Fine-tuning the Position Description

The final position description will normally run approximately three typewritten pages. Every person in the company who is involved in the hiring process, and who will ultimately sign off on a person hired to the position must be given an opportunity to review the position description, contribute to it, and approve it. There must be an agreement that this document accurately describes the position to be filled.

Nothing I have mentioned about the position description should be interpreted as meaning that once written it cannot be revised. Nothing should be thought of as cast in bronze, but use all the care and collective insight in changing it that you used in preparing it in the first place. It is almost certain that as you discuss the job with prospective employees you will want to refine the position description, which is perfectly permissible, up to a point.

Do not redefine the job to accommodate the strengths and weaknesses of a specific individual. If you do this, you will have to transfer certain responsibilities to someone else and this may create organizational chaos. If a duty or area of responsibility makes sense and logically belongs in a certain position description, leave it there and keep looking for someone who can do the whole job. No one will be 100 percent in every duty area specified and every requirement of the job. These shortfalls in knowledge, ability, or experience represent areas where the individual will be expected to grow, if hired, and where he will need support in the beginning.

It is better to leave the description intact and backstop the new hire in the areas of weakness until he gains strength than to jockey the organization around to cover permanent voids in a person's ability to do the job. As you become aware of these areas of weakness in a candidate's experience, education, or ability you have to make judgments about whether the person can and will develop in the job if hired. In this case, "can" and "will" do not mean the same thing at all. People very often do not do all they are capable of doing. Another chapter in this book deals more directly with "can" and "will" questions.

Typical Position Descriptions

Appendix A presents three position descriptions for three different management levels. They are not meant to be models and may not correspond with your concept of a president, vice president of manufacturing, or regional sales manager. Their purpose is to illustrate a typical document appropriate for use in the Critical Path Hiring method.

3
Defining the Company
Milestone B

The Critical Path Hiring method requires that the prospective management employee be an active participant in the selection process. To be assured of his/her cooperation and assistance, it is vital that the candidate's first exposures to the company be positive and that the impressions you create show that the company is a desirable place of employment. Is it necessary to treat a person who is at this point, at best, a "suspect" in such a manner? The answer is an unqualified yes. You are looking for the best possible person for the position. If you do not first share your vision of the company and its future, you will never get the opportunity to become a buyer of that person's services.

The position description explained in the previous chapter is an important tool in establishing a favorable corporate image. The company presentation is the other essential tool. This chapter defines and discusses an information package which will complement the position description.

The objectives of this information package are:

1. To provide an overview of the company's background, products, markets, organization, and structure

2. To introduce the operating philosophy of the company

3. To take positive steps toward securing the candidate's commitment to the company at the onset of employment

The information package should be carefully prepared as it will be placed in the hands of every would-be management employee. Even though only one of these people will be employed for the position in question, you will want to present the company in as favorable a light as possible. The others may some day be customers.

Fortunately, this package will not need to be prepared anew each time you need to hire a manager. It will have a lot of uses both inside and outside the hiring process.

Company Overview

Most businesses do not spring full-blown into the marketplace. They are begun and succeed because a small group of people are willing to work very hard and at considerable risk to their personal careers to make them succeed. And investors are willing to place their financial resources at risk to fund the company, based on their confidence in those people. This entrepreneurial spirit never changes in successful companies. A company's managers are its entrepreneurial custodians.

In light of this, some things you might want to describe briefly in the company overview include:

How, when, and why the company began; who founded it; how it evolved; and where it is today.

An abbreviated organizational view of the company. If the firm is a subsidiary, say how it relates to the parent. You may also want to insert an organizational view of how the management position you are seeking to fill relates to the rest of the company.

An introduction to the company's products and services. The company's advertising and promotional literature will usually fill this requirement. If the company is publicly held, an annual report should be included.

A description of how the company produces and distributes its products or services.

Any other aspects of the company and its operations which might be of interest or importance to a prospective manager.

The Corporate Operating Philosophy

Is such a document necessary? The answer to that question is probably yes. In terms of the Critical Path Hiring process, it is certainly highly desirable. This book deals with the process of selecting the best management people. It also deals with team-building. Highly qualified people are not necessarily highly motivated people, and they need to be both if they are to be the assets you are seeking. If you want a commitment to the operating goals and objectives of the company, you will have to provide something to commit to.

The hiring process is the most logical and effective place to begin to establish that commitment. Then it becomes a part of the basic agreement between the person as a manager and the company. In the previous chapter the duties and responsibilities of the management position were defined. You, of course, expect a commitment to those duties. The corporate operating philosophy defines the ethical operating environment of the company, and you will want a commitment in this area of management responsibility too.

The Ethical Framework

More and more companies are finding it necessary and desirable to publish an operating philosophy. Although such a document may be good public relations, this is not the primary purpose for which it is written. If you wish, you can assume that anyone you employ in a management position will be ethically correct in all business dealings, but careful managers should not assume anything they do not have to assume.

The statement "corporations exist to make a profit" is essentially true, but it is also a gross simplification of twentieth century American life. Its implication is that companies exist *only* to make a profit. This is, of course, patently untrue, but the assumption exists. Countless words have been written and spoken questioning business ethics, and more than a few educators in secondary schools, colleges, and universities have, often with just cause, expressed a basic distrust of corporate profit motives, operating methods, and interpersonal dealings. The statement that corporations exist to make a profit invites criticism. A better way to say it would be that corporations can't exist without profits, and their profitable existence is essential to society.

Numerous people and organizations depend on the successful operation of a company in the community.

1. *The stockholders:* On average, it requires in excess of $30,000 of investment capital to create one job. This risk capital is normally provided by stockholders. They are dependent on company management to protect and assure a fair return on their investment.

2. *The employees:* To them the company represents the means of livelihood. If it is successfully managed, the company can offer continuing employment.

3. *The customers:* They are the consumers of the goods and services the company provides.

4. *The local, state, and federal governments:* These bureaucracies are supported by tax dollars collected from the company and its employees.

5. *Banks and thrift institutions:* They provide credit to the companies and employees, but depend on those same sources for deposit dollars to create the credit.

6. *Local small businesses:* The butcher, the baker, and the candlestick maker all depend on purchases by the employees of the company.

7. *Vendors:* They are dependent on the purchase of raw materials and supplies by the company.

8. *Charities:* Contributions by the company and its employees support local and national charitable funds, churches, and nonprofit groups.

This is a lot of dependency on an organization which has no declared ethical position, no code of conduct for its business. As a matter of fact, most businesses do have an ethical framework. It just is not written down. When it is not written down, several things can happen.

The public (and the employees) may assume it doesn't exist.

Each manager could operate according to the dictates of his or her own conscience, opening the door to situation ethics.

There can be large swings in how the company relates to each of the groups depending upon it.

The company can lose an important opportunity to secure the dedication of its managers and employees.

Corporate Situation Ethics

Business ethics in this country are typically based on Judeo–Christian principles. There are two primary places where such ethics are taught—synagogues and churches. Anyone who has visited these places recently knows they are reaching a relatively small percent of the population in their formative years. Other places where one might acquire an appreciation of ethical values are the home, school, and society at large. Business ethics may be discussed at the college level but this may be done in courses designed to point out to the student what is wrong about the way companies conduct their business.

The blunt truth is that the largest percentage of the population is escaping any formal training in ethical values. While it would be wrong to imply that as a result the public is without ethical discipline, it would be equally wrong to assume that anyone who is employed in a management position will somehow acquire a fine sense of ethical judgment in the process. There is ample evidence to the contrary in the daily newspapers. Because of the multiple dependencies just mentioned, the resolution of questions involving ethical issues in business can be complex and sophisticated. When business executives flagrantly disregard the most basic ethical tenets, it breeds distrust and ill will among the public, vendors, and employees alike.

Without a published operating philosophy, the company exposes itself to situation ethics. That is to say, the decision regarding the handling of any given situation, whether it involves a customer, an employee, or anyone outside the organization, is left to the discretion of the manager involved. In actual practice what happens is this: the manager phones someone else and says, "What did we do the last time this happened?" If something comparable has happened before, there may be a section in a company policy manual to cover it. If so, the manager may be in luck. Corporate policy manuals are the common law of the company.

When there are no precedents, managers are left to decide situations based on their own innate sense of right and wrong, and their own self-interest. The corporate operating philosophy we are talking about here is not intended to replace the company policy manual. It does, however, provide the broad ethical framework within which a consistent body of company policy can develop.

Businesses do not exist primarily to build the character of their employees and those with whom they do business. They do have to be conducted on an ethical basis, however, if they are to attract and hold highly motivated, happy, productive people. The truly great companies, large and small, are also real character-builders.

Motivational Hiring

The ethical conduct of business is not the primary objective for which this book is written. Its first objective is to describe how to attract talented, motivated people to management positions. To do this, you have to provide motivators. Title, salary, and duties of the position are certainly motivators, but if you provide a set of corporate operating guidelines which make individuals feel good about the company, and perhaps even inspire them, you will have gained much more than just new managers. You may have gained disciples in the process. Those people will take pride in their place of employment and the vital role the company plays in the community. The company's problems will become their problems, and its successes will be their own. Further, as managers they will strive to instill their enthusiasm for the company in the people who work for them. Everyone needs something to believe in.

You may think that motivational hiring is a lot to expect from a simple statement of operating philosophy. Yet a carefully crafted statement can be very effective. To be sure, such a statement is not simple to write. It requires care and thought on your part. You have to believe it yourself if you want others to, and, most importantly, you have to be willing to live by it. You cannot talk ethical business practices and then not apply them.

Will it work? Thomas J. Peters and Robert H. Waterman, Jr.'s highly successful book *In Search of Excellence* glowingly describes IBM Corporation as one of the most excellent firms for the talented people it attracts and holds, for its ethical practices, for the dedication of its employees, for the imagination and quality of its products, and for the consistency of its profits.

How IBM became so good is no secret to its old-time employees. It was the work of the founder, Thomas J. Watson, Sr. From the day he started the company, he worked ceaselessly to ingrain an operating philosophy in its employees. It was a philosophy based on dignity of the individual and duty to the customer, to the other employees of the company, and to the stockholders. Over a span of almost fifty years he never missed a chance to exhort the company's employees on these values. Almost every one of his speeches which have survived consisted of two things—praise and duty. And Mr. Watson's managers followed his example, exhorting IBMers under their direct supervision on the same values.

Mr. Watson knew that if he could instill pride of IBM in its people, for how it operated and what it stood for, the people would be motivated by it. Before long, a curious thing began to happen. IBMers began to ask themselves at every turn if what they were doing served the customer, the employee, and the stockholders best. They thought about it and they tried harder, and harder, and harder. They still do.

All of this happened when IBM was a relatively small company. As late as 1950, IBM sales were only in the $215 million per year range. What has happened to IBM since then is a success story of Olympian proportions. Can it happen again? The answer to that is unquestionably yes.

One other thing needs to be said about motivational hiring. It is entirely possible to motivate people in the hiring process, but it is a lot easier if you can recognize goal-oriented people. How to do this is discussed in chapter 9.

Drafting a Statement of Corporate Operating Philosophy

Before we talk about writing a statement of corporate operating philosophy, let us consider what you're going to do with it once it is written. If it is to end up in your desk drawer, forget it. Do not even bother. It should be distributed to every manager, every employee, and everyone else the company touches. That means it should be simple and straightforward. It is possible to get by with a very brief statement, but it is of greater value to you if you view it as an opportunity to address points of concern to the company management, the employees, and the community. Here are several areas of philosophical concern which should be addressed.

Commitment to the Customer. It may seem so elementary as to be insulting to your managers' intelligence to remind them of the importance of the customer. After all, the customer's business is the life blood of the company, without which there would be no company at all. Still, it is just such a litany of priorities, beginning with the customer and repeated over and over, that contributes to the excellence of some companies. You might ask, "Do I have to say it?" The answer is yes, over and over until it conditions every action. Some people and companies lose sight of the customer. There are enough horror stories around (you can probably tell some yourself) that more should not have to be repeated here to describe what can happen when a company ignores the interests of its customers. If managers do not demonstrate strong customer orientation, will the people who report to them?

Commitment to the Stockholders. The investors put up the money that creates the jobs. It is as simple as that. So simple as to be obvious, except that it is not. The notion that corporate profits flow to a few enormously wealthy individuals is so misleading that anyone who mouths such foolishness is either deliberately trying to mislead the public or is dismally ignorant of who owns industry in this nation. Any corporation of any size has literally thousands of stockholders; some have millions. A look at who these stockholders are reveals that stock is held by the personal trust departments of banks, individual investors, funds of various types (some of which are once again held by individuals), and, importantly, pension funds, including the company's own pension fund. In the immortal words of Walt Kelly's Pogo: "We have met the enemy and he is us." The plain truth is: No return on investment, no stock value. No stock value, no credit. No credit, no company, no job, no pension, no retirement benefits, no anything. Stockholder interest is not just the president's concern. It's everyone's.

Commitment OF the Employees. The interests of the employee are inextricably interwoven with those of the customer and especially the stockholder. Additionally, *every employee has a duty and an obligation to every other employee to strengthen and preserve the means of livelihood that the company represents.* That too would seem to be obvious, but it is not. Absenteeism, employee theft, abuse of sick leave, and abuse of employee benefit programs all bear mute testimony to the fact that many people do not view these acts as crimes against fellow employees. Yet, that is exactly what they are, as well as crimes against stockholders and customers. You can construct a work ethic in your company if you will. It takes education and communication to cure the "I-only-work-here mentality."

Commitment TO the Employees. Of course, the commitment by the employee you seek will never happen unless the company also commits. The quality of life in the company is in the hands of its management. People at all levels in a company have a variety of psychic and financial needs which must be addressed if the company is to grow and prosper. Failure to recognize these needs is a passport to people problems that will not go away. Management must strive constantly to demonstrate the following:

That the company performs a useful and necessary service to its customers and, by association, to society at large

That the company operates smoothly and effectively

That the company returns a fair profit to its investors

That the company is managed in an even-handed manner

That the company rewards its workers appropriately for their efforts

That the company provides reasonable job security

That within the limits of its resources, the company is responsive to the product and service needs of the marketplace

That the employees enjoy the confidence and respect of the owners and management

That the company is a good citizen in the community and abides by the community's laws and regulations

Commitment TO the Community. Earlier in this chapter, several dependencies upon the company were described. These dependencies are very real and respect for them must be a part of the company ethos. If a community, in an effort to attract a company, arranges preferential loans, tax breaks, civic improvements, or other inducements, it does so in the expectation that the company will be a good citizen and will remain in the community at least long enough for the community to recover its investment and, hopefully, much longer. Company and community interests become intertwined and a mutual dependency develops. Both may suffer when either party defaults.

The interests of the stockholders, the customers, the employees, the company, and the community must be kept in balance and respected by all concerned. This involves ongoing communications and public relations. Problems can arise when the expectations of any of these groups exceed the ability of the company to deliver, or the company makes promises it cannot keep. Education and close communications are the only answers to the maintenance of good corporate citizenship.

It should be clear that in preparing a statement of corporate operating philosophy, the temptation to just say what sounds good should be resisted at all costs. Great care and thought should go into its preparation. It is critically important that employees and the surrounding community understand that their interests and the company's are one and the same and that if the company prospers, they may prosper too. Do not overcommit, but be positive and upbeat. There is a lot of misunderstanding and consequently mistrust of corporations on the part of communities and the public regarding just what a company can and cannot do. It needs to be clarified.

Two statements of corporate operating philosophy appear in appendix B. They reflect different management perspectives on the viewpoints just expressed, and are intended as a point of departure to begin thinking constructively about what you want to say. Each of these statements accomplishes its objective very well in my view.

4

Developing Candidate Sources

Milestone C

When Milestone A has been reached and the position defined, you can begin to develop potential candidates. You may well need a fair number of candidate-suspects because the fallout rate can be high. This is because you have defined the position narrowly in terms of skills, abilities, education, experience, and a number of other considerations, and because you are going to be highly discriminating in your selection process. Also, you will be providing candidate-suspects with a substantial amount of information about the job and the company, which will allow them to be discriminating too. Fortunately, on the positive side, people who might not normally be interested will be attracted to a well-defined position in a company that appears to be a highly desirable place of employment. Would you not be?

A variety of sources can be tapped to generate potential candidates for the management position you are seeking to fill. This chapter discusses these sources and how to approach them.

You will find that in an initial group of possible candidates, perhaps only 10 percent will merit more than preliminary consideration, and of this group only a third will end up as real contenders. If this discourages you, let us hasten to point out that you are selecting a person to manage your people, spend your money, and guide your business—successfully. That person cannot be just an average performer.

Discriminating versus Discrimination

There is a vast difference between discriminating and discrimination. Everything in this book deals with the process of being *discriminating* in the hiring process. Nothing in this book is intended to encourage the practice of *discrimination* in the hiring process. Over the past twenty years, federal equal employment opportunity laws have grown from a simple statutory commandment outlawing discrimination to a complex collection of laws, regulations, executive orders, interpretations, and court decisions. Equal employment rights have become a legal specialty and there is every reason to suspect that as time goes on this body of regulation will expand. In addition to federal regulation there are state and local laws which, in some instances, broaden the definition of discrimination and identify specific groups for protection.

As an employer, you are required to comply in full with Title VII of the Civil Rights Act of 1964 as amended, the Age Discrimination in Employment Act, and (if your organization comes under the minimum wage and hour law) the Equal Pay Act as amended. To discuss the letter of these laws is beyond the scope of this book. The spirit of these laws is to prevent discrimination in the workplace on the basis of race, color, religion, national origin, sex, age, marital status, or family responsibility. These protections apply to managerial as well as nonmanagerial personnel.

In no way does this mean that you cannot or should not be careful and selective in the employment of a manager. You must be. The successful and profitable operation of the company depends on your hiring practices. The whole purpose of the interview and evaluation process is to obtain enough information and understanding about the individual to make a valid prediction of future performance.

Candidate Sources

Candidate sources include your own organization, your circle of acquaintances, advertising, recommendations, employment agencies, placement firms, contingency search firms, internal searches, and executive search consultants. Depending on the level of the position you are seeking to fill, you may want to use any or all of them.

Sources within Your Own Organization

There are two distinct schools of thought regarding the wisdom of trying to run a management-development school within your own company. If you do it properly, after training, observing, and evaluating your students, you can promote from within with a high degree of confidence in their future performance. That is, of course, what you want—performance and predictability. How well they perform will depend on how well you have selected and trained them. If you do not do it properly—if you profess to have an unswerving policy of promoting from within and then do nothing to develop from within—you will be faced with the dilemma of having to promote people you know to be unable to perform, unable not necessarily because they can't, but because you did not prepare them.

It is primarily larger companies that can afford to set up the intermediate career paths, and provide the training and guidance involved. Unfortunately, economic conditions have forced the elimination of many middle-management positions in recent years. These positions were a sort of farm team for the majors. Now the farm team is gone.

The alternative school of thought says, "Let's stay lean and mean. If we can promote from within we will, but if no one is available with the skills and abilities we need, we'll go outside to find the right person."

You should look within your own company first. If there are no career paths to senior management, you will not be able to attract and hold high achievers. Don't, however, fall into the trap of giving old Henry a shot at the job simply because he's been around twenty-five years and has paid his dues. Do give him a shot at the job if he is qualified, but avoid the temptation to "go with the devil you know."

If the position requires a profile of skills, abilities, and experience you could not develop within your own company, you will have to go outside. You have already spent some time defining the job. You know what it needs in the way of talent. Critical Path Hiring offers a way to hire outside with confidence, but whether you promote from within or hire outside, you should use the exact same procedure to evaluate each candidate.

Sources within Your Acquaintance

How many times have you become acquainted with someone who particularly impressed you and, after careful observation over a period of time, you said to yourself, "If the opportunity comes along, I'm going to grab this person. I could use someone like that in my company."? It might be someone you've met in a charitable, church, or social activity, a tennis or golf association, or in a business setting. The person isn't exactly a friend, but something about him or her creates the impression of a valuable addition to your management team. There are no statistics on how managers employed this way work out over time.

It is not a bad way to identify possible additions to or replacements for your management organization, so long as you approach the employment process analytically. You will still need to go through the preparatory steps described in the preceding two chapters. Only then will you know exactly what you need in the way of management talent. It is also a good idea to find out who else might be attracted to the position. If the person is really right for the job, he or she won't suffer in the comparison.

Here are some things to be cautious of when employing a manager this way:

> Does the person compare favorably when the tests described later in this book are applied?
>
> Is your predisposition toward this person coloring your thinking and affecting your objectivity?
>
> You're not in the best negotiating position when you go to this person and ask him or her to consider the position. Will you end up paying more than you can afford?
>
> What if your recruit doesn't work out? Will it create problems down the road?

Gold is where you find it. These considerations shouldn't deter you from keeping a watchful eye for management talent. They should, however, be a part of your thinking when you do go about filling a responsible position this way.

Advertising

Advertising can be either local, regional, or national. The *New York Times, Chicago Tribune, Los Angeles Times* and, in fact, most large metropolitan Sunday newspapers are widely read by job seekers. The *Wall Street Journal* is capable of getting nationwide attention for your ad.

Newspaper ads will, of course, only get the attention of those who happen to be reading the "help wanted" section the day you run the ad. The cost of an ad in a national newspaper is enough to make you think twice about repeat insertions.

Advertising may or may not be effective in attracting the kind of response you would like. Some ads can turn off the very people you are trying to attract. The cliché-ridden ad in figure 4–1 is the kind you should avoid at all costs. Ads like this are a waste of time, money, and ink. They make casual ad readers laugh and serious job-seekers despair.

When you use CPH, ad writing is straightforward. You should indicate the title of the position and summarize the position overview,

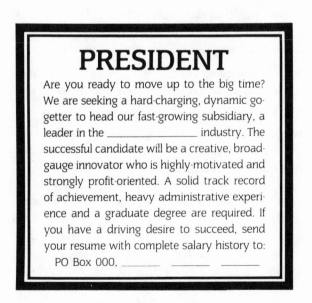

Figure 4–1. *A Money-wasting Advertisement*

the skills and abilities required, and the training, education, and experience needed for the position. These have already been established in the position description. You may or may not want to identify your company and industry. You will get a better level of response if you do. You do not normally have to describe the company in the ad. Any serious job-seeker knows how to find out about you quickly. If you are a new firm or low-visibility subsidiary of a prominent corporation, it might be appropriate to say so.

In CPH, the purpose of advertising is to solicit expressions of interest in the position. These will normally come in the form of resumes. There could be a little or a lot of response, depending on the position and where and how you advertise it. What you do with these responses is discussed in the following chapter.

Recommendations

You may wish to solicit recommendations from other executives both inside and outside your company. If you follow this route to identify prospective candidates, the correct way to proceed is as follows:

1. Make the position description available to the recommenders. Ask them to study it and to evaluate their circles of acquaintances in the light of the job requirements.

2. If they know of someone who may be qualified and interested, ask them to approach that person with the position description.

3. If the person has an interest in pursuing the opportunity, he or she should respond by letter to you, indicating interest and mentioning the recommender.

If you ask an associate, a friend, or a business acquaintance for a recommendation, you must treat it in a businesslike manner. It is very important that recommendations be handled in this way, rather than informally. They can become very touchy if handled casually by phone or over a drink in the clubhouse. Remember, there are no inside tracks or shortcuts in CPH. It is a system of hiring which must be followed faithfully with every would-be candidate at this point.

Employment Agencies, Placement Firms, and
Contingency Search Firms

All of these organizations have one thing in common—they are in the business of placing people in their client organizations. When they are successful at doing that, they are paid a fee. Usually this fee is expressed as a percentage of the starting salary of the person hired. Fees are roughly 1 percent per thousand dollars of salary up to a maximum of 30 percent of salary. These fees are often negotiable, so make your best deal at the beginning, not when you are on the hook.

To place people, you have to know people, and you have to know what jobs are in the process of being filled. People in these organizations spend a great deal of time finding out these two pieces of information. They often specialize by industry or by profession—banking, retail, publishing, accounting, data processing, and so forth. They generally know who in these industries or disciplines is susceptible to a job change and they have resumes ready when a position opportunity is identified.

As a source of people, agencies rely on quick hiring decisions, since these firms are paid only after a person is hired. If you use CPH you will be following a process which is deliberate and enforces a discipline on the placement firm as well as yourself. This is not necessarily bad because it ensures that the people they offer will get full and careful consideration. It will require that they alter their operating practices when dealing with you.

The procedure for working with placement firms is as follows.

1. Make the position description available to the firm and ask that they study it. Also explain the CPH system you are following and how candidates will be handled and evaluated.

2. Ask them to respond to you in writing with their fee structure and rates for this search.

3. Ask them to search their files to identify qualified people and to provide you with the names and addresses of individuals whom they feel might be qualified and interested in the position. This list must be in writing on the firm's letterhead.

4. Explain to the firm that you will not accept resumes from the firm and will not consider anyone unless initially brought to your attention in this manner.

5. Ask the placement firm to contact the individuals they have recommended and to review the position description with them. Any individuals having an interest should respond directly to you by letter indicating that interest, and referencing the placement firm. Such letters must come from the individuals and not the placement firm.

There is a reason for this somewhat elaborate procedure when dealing with employment agencies, placement firms, and contingency search firms. If you deal with more than one such firm in a single search activity, the same person may be referred to you by two or more agencies. If you hire that person, the firm submitting the resume to you first is entitled to the fee. You will have to sort through the lists you receive to resolve duplications. The procedure just described will protect the fee of the placement firm, and at the same time prevent you from being deluged with resumes. If you follow it you will only receive expressions of interest from sincere would-be candidates themselves and you will control the evaluation process.

Executive Search Consultant Firms

Executive recruitment can also be done by an executive search consultant. For purposes of this discussion, an executive search firm is defined as follows:

1. The organization is a management consultant group which either specializes in or has a specialty in the recruiting and selection of management personnel.

2. They should be highly professional and ethical. As with your doctor, lawyer, or accountant, you will have to pay them to provide the service for you. Their fees are approximately the same as those of placement or contingency firms. Unlike those firms, executive search consultants bill their fees *while* they are conducting the search.

3. Executive search consultants will, in their own fashion, do everything in the way of identification, screening, interviewing, evaluation, reference checking, and preselection described in this book. They then present a selection of candidates with appropriate documentation who, in their judgment, can do the job, want the job, and will be successful in the job. Your role will be one of ratification of the consultants' choices. (You should use the Critical Path Hiring procedure to make the ratification and ultimate selection.)

4. The consultant will not conduct a search if he finds that the position's duties, responsibilities, and scope of authority are not consistent with the level of the position in the organization. In other words, the job must be doable. They will also inform you if the compensation package is consistent with conditions in the job marketplace. As consultants, they will work with you to resolve problems of this sort.

5. No matter how much the position and the person being sought are discussed, the consultant will not know whether he understands your wishes until he presents a candidate and receives your evaluation. Remember, the candidate is the manifestation of your position description. You may not like what you have created. Some fine tuning is to be expected.

6. The executive search firm will not accept a fee from an individual in exchange for placement and is beholden only to the client for its fees.

7. The search consultant operates within the terms and conditions of a letter of understanding with the client. At all times it keeps the client fully informed of the progress of the search.

8. The search consultant will hold confidential all information which the client may divulge regarding the client's business activities, and will also treat with confidence information he may gain from candidates in the course of search activities.

9. The search consultant will expect to conduct your search on an exclusive basis. Any would-be candidate coming to your attention from any source at all must be referred to the search firm for evaluation.

How Search Consultants Work. But what precisely does an executive search consultant firm do? First, it researches related industries and business activities to determine where candidates can be found. Out of this initial research, a list of target companies will emerge. You should review this list. There may be some you would not want to recruit from and some which may have been overlooked by the consultant. It then identifies and discreetly contacts people at an appropriate level in the target companies to skillfully and professionally present your position and company in an attempt to stimulate the potential candidate's interest. As indicated earlier, not everyone will respond positively and, of those who do, only a small percentage will ultimately become candidates. The consultant's initial task is to stimulate interest. After successfully doing this, the consultant can stop being the seller and become the buyer.

From this point on the consultant's role is to selectively evaluate each potential candidate, maintaining and building the interest of those who are qualified, and gracefully eliminating those who are not. The consultant will visit, interview in depth, and evaluate qualified individuals. The methods and techniques the consultant uses will not differ significantly from those described in later chapters. His or her experience in using these techniques, and the insights derived from meetings with you and with the candidates, will determine how effective he or she is as an executive search consultant.

Ultimately, the consultant will select and present to you for consideration around three individuals. This presentation will first be in the form of detailed written reports on each candidate. These will be people the consultant feels: (1) are qualified, (2) are interested, (3) can be hired within the salary and other constraints of the position, and (4) if employed, will be successful in the position. Accompanying reports will tell you why the consultant believes this. The consultant will also arrange interviews, maintain liaison during your selection process, assist in negotiations, and consult with you as required to bring about a speedy conclusion of the hiring process. Remember, if you reject a candidate, you should inform the consulting firm of the reasons, in terms which will help it sharpen its perceptions of your needs. For the process to take place there has to be an exchange of information between consultant and client, and it must be in a language both understand. One of the purposes of Critical

Path Hiring is to provide a meaningful language with which to discuss a potential candidate's strengths and weaknesses.

In retaining an executive search consultant, it is vital that you have a clear understanding in the following areas:

Fees: Are they a percentage of actual or estimated salary, or are they based on total direct compensation, including estimated first-year bonuses? How and when will fees be billed?

Expenses: What expenses associated with the conduct of the search will be billed to the client?

What search cancellation privileges does the client have?

Does the consultant consider that his or her obligation is completed upon presenting candidates who are qualified in his or her opinion? Or when a candidate is actually hired?

Why Search Consultants Fail. Yes, search consultants do sometimes fail and it is not always their fault. When they fail, everyone loses, so it is worth taking a few moments to examine why it happens. The methods described in this book can forestall most but not all of the reasons a search might fail.

The principal reasons for failure are:

1. Inexperience on the part of the consultant in identifying and developing candidates

2. Not knowing what you are looking for due to, for example, a poorly defined position

3. An inconsistent position definition (a CEO with limited authority, for example)

4. Insufficient compensation for the level of the position

5. A failure to communicate between client and consultant

6. A failure to sell the company and the community as well as the position

7. Inaccessibility of the client to the consultant

8. Failure of the client to make a full disclosure of special conditions either to the candidate or the consultant

9. Attempt by the consultant to make a quick fix rather than conduct a full search

10. Inability or unwillingness of the client to reach a hiring decision

11. Failure to consider the interests of the candidate's spouse

As the saying goes, there is plenty of blame to go around. This book will help you avoid many pitfalls of hiring, while others can be minimized by starting your own search intelligently or by selecting a consultant carefully. In selecting a search firm, size does not always equate with quality. The determining factor is how good your consultant is, not how big a search firm he or she works for.

Conducting an Internal Search

The phrase *internal search* is something of a misnomer. It refers not to looking inside your own organization, but rather to the conduct of a search for qualified people in other companies, either by yourself or by another person in your own company. If you plan to employ a senior executive, you will almost certainly have to either conduct an internal search or retain an executive search consultant to conduct one for you.

Initially you may not be comfortable making direct contact with a competitor, another local firm, or another company in your industry for the purpose of attracting one of its management people to join your company. There is only one way to handle this discomfort: believe that you have an important message to communicate—a management opportunity—and that it is up to would-be candidates, not you, to determine their own interest or lack thereof.

There are forums such as business shows, trade groups, and standards committees through which you may have informal contact with other companies. Such groups may provide useful contacts which can be pursued in an internal search. There is one salient point you should remember in conducting an internal search. Whereas the people who will be contacting you with expressions of interest have one thing in common—they are interested in making a job change—the people you will be contacting in an internal search will *not* normally be considering another job. You will have to contact them by phone or letter and probe and stimulate their interest in the position you have to offer.

It is not easy to entice total strangers. You will have to present the company, the position, and the community as skillfully as you can. If the individuals you are talking to are happy with what they are doing, happy with where they are doing it, happy with what they are being paid, and happy with their future outlook, you will probably not be successful in stimulating these people's interest. On the other hand, if the seeds of discontent are present in any of these areas, they may respond to your presentation. An internal search is hard, time-consuming, and frustrating work. It is productive, however. It is an excellent (and perhaps the only) way to make highly talented and successful executives who do not read "help wanted" ads aware of the position you have to offer.

If you decide to conduct an internal search you should follow our established process to identify and develop possible candidates. Then use the CPH process to evaluate and select.

In Conclusion

All of the methods of developing candidate–suspects are designed for one purpose—to obtain expressions of initial interest to start the stream of people flowing. You do not, at this point, know if any of them are really candidates. The winnowing-out process comes later. You will have to kiss a lot of frogs to find that prince or princess.

5
Initiating the Candidate/Job Analysis Process

Milestone D

In the Critical Path Hiring process, there are suspects, and then prospects. Lastly, there are finalists. These distinctions are important because the procedures discussed in the following chapters deal with the process of narrowing down the field of contenders to a manageable few who deserve careful attention and consideration. As mentioned earlier, there are no inside tracks in CPH. Everyone is a suspect until proven a prospect.

By now, it should be apparent to even the most casual reader that the author believes the hiring of management people is serious business. The management talent that a company selects is its single greatest asset. Companies have survived and even prospered with mediocre products, and skillful, dedicated management. The converse is rarely true.

How to Handle Expressions of Interest

As a result of your advertising or other means of priming the pump described in the previous chapter, expressions of interest should be either trickling or, hopefully, pouring in. You are going to need a lot of them. The methods of developing candidates described in chapter 4 are designed to produce written responses but, whether written or verbal, they should be logged in by date with some indication made of how each is handled.

In the management selection and employment process, it is just good business practice to be able to recall and reconstruct how and why you disposed of each suspect, prospect, or finalist. CPH lends itself to this sort of orderly procedure because it is a disciplined approach which generates a good deal of specific information about the individuals and their qualifications for a position. When you go public with your needs through advertising or other means, you really go public. If anyone who responds should later on feel short-changed in the selection process and decide to do something about it, the ability to reconstruct your decision could be invaluable. Hiring is judgmental, but judgments can be questioned. If anything in this respect is going to happen, it will probably occur within nine months of the hiring process.

Some initial screening is possible and necessary. If you advertise, you will surely receive responses that fail to cross your threshold of acceptability. A brief but polite letter of acknowledgment and rejection is the professional way to handle these inquiries. Those responses which merit further consideration should receive a mailed information package and, if possible, a telephone call.

The Information Package

Provide each respondent with a package containing:

1. A cover letter of acknowledgment
2. The position description
3. The company information folio
4. Instructions on how to proceed with job applications

The instruction set should include a request that individuals study the job and the company information carefully. Those people wishing to pursue the position should complete the forms enclosed and return them to you. The forms should include:

1. A data-capture form for detailing past educational experience and a chronological record of all past work experience.

2. A sample format for a written response concerning every duty and responsibility in the position description. The format

should enable candidate-suspects' to express their ability to meet the requirements.

3. A request for a brief biographical sketch of the person.

This may seem like a lot of writing and thought to ask of an individual so early in the process, but there are sound reasons behind it. You need the information requested in order to do a preliminary screening and allow you to zero in on the legitimate suspects.

What You've Accomplished So Far

As people respond to your request, it's clear that several important goals have been reached.

1. Candidates have studied the job requirements in the context of their own abilities and interests.

2. They have learned something about the company and what will be expected of them.

3. They have made a psychological commitment as well as investments of time and attention to give you what you've asked for.

4. You can see how well they express themselves in writing.

5. You may be able to sense the urgency people attach to their inquiries.

You must study the information provided to determine if people in fact meet the requirements of the job and should be interviewed. You now have something solid to base that decision on.

You may be saying to yourself: "Do I have to go through all this for every applicant? After all, I'm not hiring the president of the company." We can't tell you how important each manager is, but here's something to consider. If you have nine managers, the next one you hire is 10 percent of your team. In professional football, it is critical that you have eleven men on the field at all times, that they are the best eleven you can get, and that their performance is predictable. If you don't do this, you will be scored upon. It is also true in business.

Critical Path Hiring takes time and effort. There is no way to avoid that and still get the required results. Someone has to do it. It is possible, depending on the size of the company to delegate some of the work. But in the final analysis, if you want to know who your managers are and whether they are the right people, you will have to be a part of the hiring process.

Elements of the Application

The Chronological Record

The chronological record is a vital component of any application. But why do you want it in the first place? Why not just use the individual's resume? It is true that a resume should contain the same information but there are as many different types of resumes as there are people, and most resumes are condensed in one way or another. Some are not even written by the people they describe. Resumes are also sales brochures. And, let's face it—the attractiveness and readability of a resume can sometimes overshadow the information it contains. Anyone who has sat and read resumes all day knows that after about the first hour your brain is numb. You tend to sort out the more readable ones for closer consideration. That is when the romancing begins, and one of the objectives of CPH is to take the emotion out of hiring a manager. Not put it in.

The most important reason for the chronological record is to establish accurate dates of every bit of training and work experience the individual possesses. In addition, it is to capture what is important *to you* about the person's experience. If you provide the sample form shown in appendix C, you will have a good chance of getting the information you need. It is absolutely essential that you get this information. All of it.

The chronological-data-capture form should request the following:

1. *Name and current address and telephone number.*

2. *Education:* What schools, dates attended, courses pursued, and degrees conferred, or graduation achieved.

3. *Special education and training:* Courses and seminars, with subject matter and dates.

4. *Work experience:* Every job ever held after completion of education, with dates, employer, location, title, duties, accomplishments, and compensation progression. No period in the individual's adult life should be unaccounted for.

5. *Activities:* Leisure interests, community involvement, and so forth.

6. *Special skills and abilities:* Languages, music, and art, for example. Identify special achievements, awards, and recognition.

7. *Personal data:* Marital status, children, and so forth.

The Biographical Sketch

You may think that the biographical sketch is the least important and most dispensable piece of information you are requesting. Actually, it is vitally important to a balanced and fair evaluation of the individual. In CPH, it is essential that you get to know the person you are hiring. How that person got where he or she is today can provide critical insights into motivation, value system, and personal goals. You cannot practice the "paper bag over the head" philosophy when you are employing managers. They will be managing the employees of the company, dealing with the customers, and representing the company to the general public and community. It is not fair to the individual or to any of these groups not to look at the whole person.

Some respondents will do a better job than others in putting together a biographical sketch. Most managers understand the importance of the sketch and will do their best. However, modesty is still viewed by some as a virtue and you will later have to supplement what they provide in these cases, if you feel it necessary for a thorough and complete understanding of the person. Do not pry!! You will know quickly if you are in danger of invading the individual's privacy. Respect that privacy.

Duty and Responsibility Responses

You have provided the suspect with a carefully prepared position description which, among other things, spells out the key duties and responsibilities of the position. The individual should study these requirements in the context of his or her education and work experience, industry knowledge, and administrative skills and abilities. By asking suspects to comment on each requirement, you will force them to do some self-analysis and introspective thinking about the position and the commitment it requires. That is, of course, what you want to happen.

You should also provide a form to solicit these responses. The form should look something like the one shown in appendix C. How coherent and articulate these responses are will be a big help in reaching the next two milestones in the CPH process with the individual. It is also essential that you get this information.

What You've Accomplished

At this point, you have accomplished several important things:

1. You have treated each respondent in the same nondiscriminatory, evenhanded manner.

2. You have given respondents an accurate detailed statement of the job they will be expected to perform.

3. You have given them a statement of what the company they may be working for is all about, what its goals and objectives are, what its products are, and anything else about the company's operations you believe a prospective manager should know.

4. You have set the stage for a meaningful interview.

The Problem of Missing Data

Some of the people you send the package to will not respond with the information you request. This should not be too great a disappointment. In addition to informing the suspects, you are also prequalifying them for further consideration. How you develop candidates for the position will also enter into consideration. If you are using advertising or a placement firm, the expressions of interest you receive tell you that the individuals are receptive to a job change. If the position you have to offer is a better one than they now have (or if they are currently unemployed), and often, whether they feel qualified or not, they will give you what you ask.

On the other hand, if you are relying on recommendations or conducting a search, you may have to work harder to obtain this vital data. If the position is clearly a step up for the individual and you've done a good job of selling the company, he or she may comply. Some individuals need some wooing, however; here you will have to drag the information out of them. (This is one of the things that search consultants do for you.)

CPH is not a passive system from the would-be candidates' point of view. It is designed to get them involved in the evaluation and selection process. If you are successful in this you will have willing and cooperative suspects or prospects with whom you can have frank, open and mutually beneficial discussions. It may be difficult to do this when the person is not actively seeking an employment change. It is by no means impossible, however. If you do not believe you can ask the person to provide this information at this stage, you will have to gain it later on in the interview process. Either way, you must get it and, when you do, you should use the standard forms to write it down.

The Inquiry You Didn't Ask For

Generally, this book deals with the process of filling an identified management position. When such a need becomes evident, the requirement is broadcast by the means discussed in the preceding chapter, and the CPH method is employed to hire a manager. But what do you do when there is an individual and no identified position?

On occasion, a skilled and experienced executive will contact you (or a member of your board or another senior executive in your organization), and express an interest in joining your company. This individual may or may not be personally known to you. If others in your organization know the person, there could be extreme pressure to find a place for him or her. Often the individual in question meets this profile:

1. A skilled and experienced manager

2. A highly successful track record

3. Industry-knowledgeable and/or possessing valuable industry awareness or contacts

4. Socially well-connected and prominent

5. Expensive

It would be useless, and possibly ill advised, to suggest that you not consider this person. It would be just as ill advised, however, to hire the individual without an identified position in mind. If there is no identified need, you will have to do the following:

1. Review your own management staff to determine if anyone can or should be displaced from an identified position.

2. Failing that, consider the possibility of reorganizing in such a way as to create a suitable position.

3. Consider the compensation requirements of the individual and its impact on existing compensation levels of other executives in your organization.

4. If you can assimilate him or her, use the CPH method to define the position and evaluate the person. By so doing, whether you employ the individual or not, you will know unequivocally that you have done the right thing. And you will be able to prove it.

There is room for serious reflection on whether any long-term benefit to the company can derive from bringing a senior executive into an organization in a position junior in authority, span of control, or compensation to the one the person previously held. That individual has been calling the shots and may have difficulty accepting the managerial authority constraints which the lower-level position represents. If you should bring someone into the company under such circumstances, it is essential that all of the milestones in CPH be touched in the hiring process. Especially important is a critical look at the psychic (nonmonetary) needs and rewards which the individual derives from work, as discussed in chapter 9. Failure to touch this base could result in bringing into your organization a source of divisiveness rather than the asset you perceive.

Having voiced this "caveat," it is also appropriate to point out that there are many "senior statesmen" of business available in every management discipline (and there will be more) whose knowledge and experience can be tapped by the astute manager. These people, who have come to terms with their contending interests and other constraints and want to cycle down, can be tremendously helpful as retained consultants. They can multiply a busy executive's presence and provide a closer focus on problems than might otherwise be possible. No less care should be exercised in selecting these people than in hiring a full-time executive, and CPH can also be used in this process.

6
Identifying Possible Candidates
Milestone E

B y now your efforts to locate candidates have begun to bear fruit. Expressions of interest are flowing to you from a variety of sources and you are responding with the materials and procedures described in chapter 5. Suspects' reactions to the receipt of your information package are fairly predictable. They are a little overwhelmed. It has been the author's experience that when this type and amount of information is placed into the hands of prospective management employees, they read it very, very carefully.

Your objective has been to present to the candidate-suspects a clear, detailed picture of what kind of company you are, what kind of job this is, and what will be expected of them in the position. It will be a refreshing change from the ordinary for these people, and it will create a positive impression of the importance you attach to the position, the employee, and the company. It will also make clear that applicants wishing to pursue the opportunity must become actively involved in the hiring process. They will have to study the materials provided and then make a conscious decision as to whether or not to respond. If the decision is positive, they will have to do a little work to provide the response information you've requested.

But will their decisions be positive? Will enough people respond to make the Critical Path Hiring process work? This hinges on three things: (1) the level of the position in the organization, (2) the compensation offered, and (3) how widely you publicize your need—how wide a net you cast for candidates. Or expressed another way, the unique combination of skills and abilities you are seeking, and how scarce or abundant that combination is in the management marketplace.

The purposes of requesting the candidate suspect to supply the biographical, education, and work experience chronology are to save time, and to secure an initial psychological commitment from the person.

The Telephone Follow-up

Depending on the time constraints under which you are operating and the volume of response, you may want to follow up on your mailing with a personal phone call. If you do it will enhance the quantity and possibly also the quality of the responses you get to your information requests. This telephone follow-up does not necessarily have to be done by you personally, but it will be a lot more effective and productive if it is.

Don't underestimate the impact of your personal phone call asking if the would-be candidate has received the materials you've mailed, and requesting that he or she fill in the required forms as quickly as possible. It is flattering to the applicant and also lends a note of urgency and importance to the information you requested.

At this point, you should avoid any discussion of the position—it is much too early for that. One call should be sufficient. If it does not elicit the information, one of two things has probably occurred: (1) the would-be candidate has read the materials and isn't interested, or (2) he or she doesn't feel qualified. Either way, you should scratch that name off your list.

CPH presumes you will be developing candidates by the methods described in chapter 4. You can expect that prospective candidates developed this way will have an initial interest in the position and respond accordingly. If, however, you are conducting an internal search, another approach is required. You will be identifying and contacting people who are *not* thinking of a job change. They will have to be contacted initially by telephone and then personally, and you will probably have to fill out the preliminary forms in the previous chapter yourself either during or after an initial interview. Once you have done that, the normal CPH procedure can be pursued.

Setting up the Candidate File

The candidate file is essential to an orderly review of each person's qualifications. In the hiring process, information about a candidate and copies of correspondence can become scattered. When this happens it becomes very difficult to control the process, and control is the essence of CPH. There must be a specific file where a record of all exchanges with each candidate are kept so all information received from the person and generated through meetings with him or her can be located quickly. This file becomes especially important when more than one person (a search committee for example) must meet, interview, and evaluate the candidate. As the hiring process progresses, a considerable amount of information will accumulate. At this point in the process the candidate file might contain:

1. Letter(s) of recommendation

2. The candidate's inquiry letter and/or resume in response to an ad

3. The recommendation reference from an agency

4. A copy of the cover letter sent with the information package to the candidate

5. The candidate's responses (biographical sketch, chronology of education and work experience, and responses to the duties and responsibilities section of the position description)

There is another reason to keep an individual file on each candidate. All hiring is judgmental. If you should ever be called upon to explain or defend why you did or did not hire a specific person, as is sometimes required in the public as well as the private sector, you will be able to reconstruct the decision quickly and completely through the CPH candidate file.

We live in a highly litigious society where almost any decision in business or the public domain can be questioned in a court of law. You may even be called upon to demonstrate that over a period of years you have conducted the hiring process in a totally fair and evenhanded manner. But hiring is by definition selective and judgmental. If you cannot reconstruct the hiring decision you will not be able to defend your judgments.

As you begin the screening-out process, exercising your responsibility to select the best individual for your company, you will be closing a number of candidates' files. Store these files!!! Do not throw them away. The cost of storage is nothing compared to the cost of legal counsel and lost time away from the job, which you will incur in trying to build a defense without adequate records. The stakes are very high. It could cost you tens or hundreds of thousands of dollars if a judge or jury should find for the plaintiff, and cost thousands more in a tarnished corporate image.

Preinterview Screening

A good case can be built for doing as much preinterview screening as possible. As mentioned in the previous chapter, some who respond to your ad will not cross your threshold of acceptability and will be screened out at that point. In reaching milestone E you will be able to perform a second level of screening based on the information contained in the responses the candidates have provided. If you have not asked them to send you this information in advance of scheduling the first interview, you will, of course, not be able to do this screening, and will have to schedule the first interview based on whatever information is available. This data will typically come from a resume, and a resume is a notoriously bad document on which to base a decision to spend several hours of your and other executives' time, not to mention the possible costs of travel and overnight accommodations which the visting candidate will incur, and which you will probably reimburse.

The Trouble with Resumes

Numerous books advise job-seekers on how to write a sales brochure describing themselves as the product. Each of these books provides at least a half-dozen resume formats to choose from. Since resumes are designed to emphasize strengths and interests while minimizing weaknesses, and because they are seldom written in response to a specific job description and requirement, it is very difficult to make a judgment from them about how a candidate would fill your specific needs. You know, in using CPH, what your specific needs are, but the candidate did not know those needs when writing the resume.

Some resumes are deliberately truncated, on the assumption that if they are long and detailed, they won't be read. Sometimes they are painfully shortened to one page, even for an experienced executive. Others attempt to synopsize skills, abilities, education, and experience separately from work experience; reduce the employment record to company name only; or merely include job title. Still others provide no chronology of job tenure, or do not even list all jobs held, making it impossible to draw any conclusions about continuity of employment. Add to this the job-seeker's option to print the resume on anything from 5-lb. tissue to 80-lb. card stock and in any color of the rainbow, and you have a difficult document on which to make a value judgment.

Critical Path Hiring, by using a standardized chronology format, forces the candidate to give you the information you need in the form and level of detail necessary to make some preliminary observations.

There is another advantage to using this CPH format. In the course of the hiring process you may be contacting possible candidates who do not have up-to-date resumes. Depending on their level of interest they may not be willing or able to take the time to perform this update. Writing a resume is fairly traumatic for many people. They want to put their best foot forward, but they are not sure how to do it. The CPH format makes this process less intimidating.

You are now at the point where you are going to decide whom you will interview for the position in question. Interviewing takes time, and as mentioned earlier, it may also be expensive to bring people to your offices. Before doing so, for each respondent you will have to carefully read three key documents: the chronological record, the commentary on duties and responsibilities, and the biographical sketch. The time to do it is now, not when the individual is walking through your door.

Reviewing the Chronological Record

Here are some things to look for in the chronological record.

General issues:

Did the respondent follow your instructions? Are the forms reasonably complete? Do they indicate that some care and thought went into their preparation? Or is the response thrown together?

Does the response indicate that the candidate–suspect read and understands the materials you've provided?

Are the responses reasonably literate? Do they indicate acceptable written communications skills and a command of business English? Do they show an ability to articulate feelings, attitudes, and opinions?

Are there any significant gaps in the candidate's chronology of education and work experience? Is all time accounted for?

Type and amount of education:

Have the base-line educational requirements of the position been met?

Has the person demonstrated an interest and willingness to keep his or her education current through seminars, conferences, postgraduate study, and specialized sales, computer, or other job-related training programs?

Job tenure:

What sort of staying power does the work-experience chronology demonstrate? What is the average length of time per employer?

Does the work-experience chronology indicate that the candidate is increasing or decreasing in capability?

Has the person progressed to more responsible positions with previous employers? Is a record of promotion evidenced?

Scope of responsibility:

Do the job responsibilities of each position fit the titles?

Have past positions offered the opportunity to develop the management skills needed in the position you are seeking to fill?

Has the individual been exposed to the required areas of functional responsibility embodied in the position applied for?

Accomplishments:

Is the individual able to articulate what was accomplished in past jobs?

Do these accomplishments seem reasonable in the light of the position held, the scope of responsibility, and the time in the position?

Are they impressive?

Compensation:

Do levels of compensation in past jobs seem reasonable?

Did the individual improve his or her compensation in job changes?

Is the individual's compensation level consistent with the job you are seeking to fill?

Reviewing the Duties and Responsibilities Commentary

Preparation of the chronology is a fairly straightforward task for would-be candidates. They may have to reconstruct what seems like ancient history in the way of dates and activities, but with a little thought and research, it can be accomplished. Preparing the commentary on the duties and responsibilities of the position, however, is more challenging. Individuals will have to consider their own work experience carefully, and assess how it has prepared and qualified them to deal with the duties and responsibilities of the job you have identified. They will then have to articulate their competence in the forms which you have provided.

Appendix C includes a sample response form for comments on the duties and responsibilities of the position. It dedicates a full page for the respondent's comments on each duty. You must read these comments carefully and make an initial judgment for each duty as to whether or not you concur. The last line on the page is the rating line.

0   5   10

As you review the comments, give the individual a preliminary evaluation or score on each duty.

Reviewing the Biographical Sketch

The purpose of the biographical sketch is to give you an initial understanding of the would-be candidate as a person. It is not a document on which you would base a judgment of whether you would or would not interview the person. Later on in the interview process you will gain a good deal more information about the candidate's personality, needs, interests, and value system. You will want to gain some insights into what experiences have shaped those qualities. The odds are you won't learn much of that by reading the biographical sketch, especially if the applicant is shy or modest. What you may gain, however, are some hooks which will lead you into areas of discussion with the person later on, and these discussions could be revealing.

Scheduling the First Interview(s)

Now you have the information and the observations needed to perform another level of screening. If the information indicates that the individual appears qualified, it is time to schedule the first face-to-face interview. Typically, what will happen is that some individuals will be clearly qualified, some will be marginal, and some respondents will be just as clearly unqualified. The unqualified ones should be quickly and politely notified of your decision, and their files closed. Closed does not mean thrown away!

Begin by scheduling interviews with those who appear to be best qualified. There will not normally be a lot of these. It is not unusual to send out a hundred information packages and end up with only a half-dozen people who appear fully qualified. With CPH, however, you will have a high level of comfort that the six or so you do have are, in fact, worth talking to. Hold the marginal ones in reserve until you've held initial interviews with the first group. You will know by then if you'll need the others.

Don't be too dismayed at the fact that you have sent out perhaps a hundred packages of information and received only a few responses in return. What you have done is place a carefully conceived presentation of your company into the hands of a hundred or so would-be managers, who have probably read it carefully. That is good public relations at the very least.

To sum up, the purpose of this chapter is to explain the candidate-qualification work that must be done in advance of an actual face-to-face meeting. If you do this preinterview screening carefully, you will accomplish the twin objectives of saving some of your time by not talking to those respondents who are unqualified or only marginally qualified, and you will at the same time get to know something about those you do want to talk to. So, do your homework.

7
The First Interview(s)
Milestone F

For the first time you are eyeball to eyeball with the candidate. Notice that the candidate is no longer a suspect, but has advanced to the level of prospect. You already know a good deal about this person, who in turn knows a good deal about your company. The stage has been set for a productive discussion of common interests. What the candidate-prospect does not know is how careful and thorough you are going to be. In all probability, the candidate will not have experienced an interview process as comprehensive as this one, and it may take a little time for him to adjust to the level of detail involved. Most candidates enjoy it once they are into it. They know they are being fully considered. There is nothing more depressing to candidates than to come out of an interview knowing that they have not been asked the right questions and wondering what the hiring decision will be based on. You are going to ask the right questions.

The first interview may, in fact, be a series of interviews, as many meetings with the candidate-prospect as are required to accomplish four goals.

1. Satisfy yourself, through careful questioning, that you thoroughly understand the individual's educational background.

2. Satisfy yourself, through careful questioning, that you thoroughly understand the individual's record of employment.

3. Agree or disagree with the candidates' statement of why he or she is qualified to perform each duty and responsibility of the position.

4. Answer thoroughly the candidate's questions about the position and the company in general.

To accomplish these goals, you will have to seize and maintain control of the interview. You will also have to make an organized set of notes on the interview which you can review and evaluate later. The best approach is to compartmentalize the interview into the four above areas. Do not go on to the next area of questioning until you are comfortable that you have enough information to form a solid opinion.

Scheduling the Interview

Interviewing is emotionally tiring for the candidate as well as for yourself. It may, in fact, be so stressful that you will not want to do it for more than two hours a day, and then preferably in the morning when you and the candidate are both fresh. The reason for the stress on your part is that you will be orchestrating and controlling the interview to maximize the flow of pertinent information from the candidate. You will have to listen carefully to the candidate's responses, hanging on every word to be sure you understand. You will also be observing how the candidate answers the questions and reacts to the questioning process. You will want to take note of the candidate's reactions to the interview, as commented upon later in this chapter.

It is essential that you guard against interruptions when you are conducting an interview. Dispose of the "crisis du jour" beforehand, so that intrusions by your secretary, the telephone, or others will not occur to interrupt your concentration or the flow of information. Interruptions should be initiated by you to break the tension, or to change to another line of questioning.

Be sure the candidate is as comfortable and relaxed as possible. Candidates too are under a considerable amount of stress. They do not know what to expect in the way of questions, or what sort of responses you are looking for. All they know at this point is that they have an interest in the company and the position, as it has been presented to them. They are hoping that you will ask the right kind of questions—ones that will allow them to put their best foot forward. Up to a point, you should not disappoint them. They will be demonstrating strengths and minimizing weaknesses. You will be looking for strengths also, but at the same time trying to accurately assess the importance of the very weaknesses they are attempting to hide.

Controlling the Interview

In any interview situation, someone is in control. It must be you if you are to make the observations and evaluations described in this book. If you do not, you will conclude interviews without enough information about candidates to make an informed judgment of whether they can do the job—and that is the whole objective of the first interview(s). A number of methods and devices can be employed to help you gain and hold control of the interview. It has been said that most candidates are accepted or rejected in the first five minutes of an interview. You cannot hire management people this way. You must get all of the pertinent information and make all of the necessary observations, and you must defer a decision until you have done so.

Just about every book on how to find a job tells the job-seeker to be warm, friendly, and outgoing in the interview situation. The premise is that warm and friendly people are more likely to be hired. It is, of course, good advice—if you are looking for a job. If, however, you are managing a business and you allow your personal attraction to a candidate to be too great a factor in the hiring decision—to cloud your ability to accurately judge how well someone meets the job's requirements—neither of you will emerge the winner. The candidate may end up being hired, but will not ultimately enjoy your confidence.

Do not misunderstand. Personal chemistry—the interaction between people which enables them to work together sympathetically and effectively, and with high, sometimes inspired, productivity—is undeniably important. It is, however, much more than a question of pleasing personalities. Your comfort level with a prospective manager is a consideration in hiring, but it is only one of many.

You can control the emotion inherent in the interview process by following the four-point format mentioned above. The candidates have provided you with education and work chronologies, and with their assessments of their ability to do the job. Do not ask any questions in this part of the interview process which do not focus on verification and understanding of this information. If the candidate attempts to deflect this line of questioning, you should politely interrupt and redirect his or her responses.

Interviewing Techniques and Considerations

Since there are already excellent books on the subject of interviewing, it is not the purpose of this book to instruct in this area. A few hints and pointers, however, may be useful.

1. Do not ask questions which elicit one-word answers.

2. Do not ask candidates to tell you about themselves. If you do, you will be turning control of the interview over to them. You could have trouble getting it back. There will be plenty of opportunity in the second set of interviews for candidates to talk about themselves.

3. Use the "echo questioning" technique. You can seek clarification and amplification of a candidate's statement by repeating it with a questioning inflection.

   CANDIDATE: I took over a losing division of the company and turned a $50,000 loss into a $250,000 profit in one year.

   INTERVIEWER: You turned a $50,000 loss into a $250,000 profit in one year?

4. Probing is a method of taking apart a candidate's pat statement and analyzing it bit by bit.

   CANDIDATE: I introduced a new cost-accounting system which had a dramatic and positive effect on company profits.

   INTERVIEWER: Describe the old system, the one you replaced. . . . How did you go about the definition and development of the new system within your company? . . . What sort of problems did you have in selling and installing the new system within your company? . . . What effect did the new system have on product-pricing? . . . What was the effect on profits?

   Probing is a useful tool for determining the extent of a candidate's involvement in and knowledge of a subject. It is not uncommon for people to take credit for achieving something almost singlehandedly when in fact they were only marginally involved.

5. Some candidates, especially the experienced ones, are skilled at getting the interviewer to talk about the company or themselves. Then they just sit back and listen. Beware of this! You will not learn anything about the candidate while you are talking, so resist at all costs the urge to make a speech. Also, do not attempt to sell candidates on the job and company at this point. You have already provided them with a lot of information, and you can assume they have a certain level of interest from their compliance with the preinterview procedure.

6. Watch body language—eye, hand, and foot movements and other nonverbal cues which can provide insight into how the candidate is reacting to you and your questions. Depending on the sophistication of the candidate and the stress of the situation, body language can either tell you a lot or nothing at all. Some nervousness is to be expected in initial interviews, but this should abate somewhat as the process proceeds. If you are a student of body language, you can place an appropriate value on it. If not, do not overrate it—it is easy to misread.

7. Do not use trick questions. Asking candidates to define the law of supply and demand or to solve a problem in abstract logic qualifies as cruel and unusual treatment. They are under a considerable amount of stress—far in excess of what is encountered in day-to-day business—so responses to such questions will tell you very little about their ability to do the job.

8. Do not ask long, drawn out questions. Keep them brief and sharply focused. If you do this, you will stand a much better chance of getting specific responses. You will also gain an impression of the candidate's ability to focus on a specific point of information, and to give you a concise response.

9. Do not ask candidates to describe their strengths and weaknesses. At the conclusion of the first interview(s) you may know their strengths far better than they can articulate them, and even if they admit privately to any weaknesses, they probably are not

going to confess them to you. You will have pinpointed those weak areas anyhow, if you follow the interview strategy described in this chapter.

It is a fact that if you ask the right questions, listen carefully, and observe closely, sooner or later most candidates will tell you what you want to know. So allow enough time for that to happen. If you are friendly and do not project the image of being judgmental, you will be successful in relaxing candidates and establishing an environment in which a full and free flow of information can take place. There is an easy way to do this—just be interested in each candidate as a person. He or she will detect it instantly.

Privacy and Discrimination: Two Sensitive Issues

To predict an applicant's potential, you will have to get to know that person and, since interviews are essentially question-and-answer periods, you will have to ask the prospective manager a series of questions on a wide range of subjects. So long as those questions focus on the ability of the individual to do the job, you should have no trouble. You must approach the interview as a frank and honest discussion to determine if the individual is right for the position, and if the position is right for the individual. You should assure interviewees that they have the right to refuse to answer any question which they feel might violate their privacy, or elicit information which could be used to discriminate against them under any aspect of the Civil Rights Act or any other rule. If they do choose to not answer a question for these reasons, you must respect their right to privacy. Further, you must not allow a refusal to influence your overall judgment of the person in the context of the job opportunity.

Discussing the Educational Experience

You have asked candidates to describe their total formal education experience, including secondary, college, specialized industry, and business-skills-development training. Presumably they have provided you with a fairly detailed accounting of this experience. In the first interview session(s), you will want to gain an understanding of these credentials and some feel also for their quality and the candidates' initiative in gaining them.

Most position descriptions carry a statement of the minimum educational requirement for the position, but there is often room for a good deal of latitude in interpreting the sufficiency of an individual's education. If you have stated unequivocally that an undergraduate degree from an accredited college or university, and/or an M.B.A. or other graduate degree is a baseline requirement, then you will have to eliminate from consideration anyone who does not possess such credentials. You can easily do this before beginning the interview process. If you have not been so unequivocal and have added "or equivalent experience" to the educational-requirement statement, you will have given yourself the opportunity to be a little flexible in interpreting the requirement. Sometimes otherwise highly qualified people are dismissed from consideration or discouraged from even applying for a position because of inflexible educational requirements.

There are an almost infinite number of educational possibilities:

1. The high school graduate who is an enormously effective and successful manager

2. The M.B.A.-holder from a prestigious university who is not an effective manager

3. The holder of a degree completely alien to his or her field of work

4. The person who earned a degree by attending night school for many years

5. The person who is still attending night school to earn a degree

6. The holder of several undergraduate degrees but no graduate degree

7. The quality of the degree (all M.B.A.s are not equal, but then all students in the same M.B.A. program do not emerge equally qualified either)

In Critical Path Hiring, education is one, but only one, of the bases for evaluating candidates' performance potential. It may not even be an important one. If you allow room for your own judgment in evaluating the adequacy of their education, you will impose upon yourself the necessity to learn something about their educational experience. That will take some effort on your part. At the same time, however, you will avoid the possibility of arbitrarily screening out a highly qualified super-achiever who could benefit your management team, but lacks impressive diplomas. You may also avoid an expensive and potentially embarrassing discrimination lawsuit.

Certain lines of questioning will provide insight into the value of a candidate's education. These should start the information flowing, and you can probe as deeply as you feel necessary to reach an opinion of whether the educational requirement is met.

1. How did you select your course of study at Old Siwash?

2. How did you fund your college education?

3. What nonacademic activities did you participate in? How did they impact your studies and grades?

4. What grade point average did you achieve?

5. What courses did you enjoy most? Least?

6. Were you awarded any scholarships? Or serve as a teaching assistant?

7. What was your thesis subject? Was it published?

8. How would you evaluate the quality of instruction at Old Siwash?

9. Have you kept in touch with any of your professors?

10. If you could relive that experience, what would you do differently?

11. What was the most valuable thing you gained from your educational experience?

12. Why didn't you complete your degree program? (if applicable)

It is important to point out that the detail of the response you receive to questions like these will depend to some extent on how far removed from college or other educational experiences candidates are, and what importance they themselves attach to them. If they are vague or uncommunicative about schooling, or ask why you are pursuing that line of questioning, you can say it is to gain a better understanding of their career development—and that is precisely the truth.

In addition, there are all sorts of noncollegiate educational opportunities which an individual might pursue. These include courses in selling, public speaking, special industry training, management, business law, computers, and stress management, to name only a few. You will want to identify and explore these areas of candidates' educational experience also.

Lastly, you will want to establish precisely, in the case of colleges or universities attended and degrees indicated, the dates and degrees conferred. You will need this information to confirm the credentials. In most cases, the registrar or some other college official will confirm the degree. For more detailed information, you will probably have to obtain the candidate's written authority to release the data. You should, in any case, verify information on the candidate's chronology before hiring.

Discussing the Record of Employment

One of the most reliable indicators of future performance is past performance. But, if you do not take the time and trouble to really understand an individual's work experience, you will not learn if that person has acquired the skills and knowledge to do the job you are seeking to fill. The record of employment can tell you a lot about the candidate. Here are some general things to look for.

Completeness. Is every job the candidate has held since entering the work force shown? You will want to know about every one, not just the most recent. To be sure, the more recent ones are the most important, but you need to know about growth and career development. Where multiple jobs with the same employer are indicated, they should be looked at as though they were with different employers. Advancement within a company is important, but so is the experience gained in each job. Further, you should establish the starting and termination dates of each job to the month, and satisfy yourself that there are no significant gaps in the record. If there are, find out why they occurred.

Job tenure. If there are frequent job changes with short tenure, look for:

Personality and attitude problems

Drinking problems

Health problems

Unrealistic work expectations

Family problems

Financial problems

Some people exhibit a propensity to change jobs every three, four, or five years. This does not really qualify as short job tenure, but it does tell you something. If the pattern is set, it will probably happen in your employ too. Sometimes this is a means of "ratcheting up" income, and/or leap-frogging to higher levels of management responsibility. It can be useful to know to what drum an individual is marching.

For every position the candidate has held, you should establish and understand the following:

1. Name and location of employer

2. Dates of employment

3. Position(s)

4. Duties and responsibilities

5. What the candidate feels he or she accomplished in the position

6. What he or she enjoyed most and least about the position

7. How the candidate related to people above, at the same level, and below him or her in the organization

8. The management system used by the employer

9. The candidate's compensation progression in the job

10. Reasons for leaving the company

When exploring the duties and accomplishments the candidate has stated, be sure to ask not only what was done but how it was done. You will be looking for the development of management skills and abilities the candidate will need in the position for which you are interviewing. The techniques described earlier will help you probe these subjects.

Discussing Duties and Responsibilities

In the previous chapter, you made some initial observations about the candidates' ability to perform the duties of the position, and recorded this information on a rating line for each duty. Now you can gain a lot more information with which to sharpen those ratings. At this point in the first interview(s), you should discuss each duty and responsibility with the candidates. You will want comments on the following:

1. Has he or she performed the duty or carried the responsibility in a previous position?

2. What, in past work, education, or life experience, qualifies them to perform the duty effectively?

3. Do they enjoy doing that sort of work?

4. Have they been successful in the performance of the duty in the past?

These duties are what the person will be doing on a day-to-day basis in the position and the measures by which overall performance will be evaluated. As you discuss the individual duties with candidates, refine your ratings. No one will rate a "10" on every duty and responsibility. These ratings will tell you where candidates' strengths and weaknesses are, where they will be expected to grow, and where support and assistance may be required.

At the conclusion of this part of the first interview(s), you will have completed a fairly analytical evaluation of the candidates' ability to do the job. Further, if others have followed a similar procedure, you will be able to compare notes and ratings. Ordinarily, you would not carry on such a critical interview process, with three or more people interviewing the candidate in such depth, unless it were for a senior management position. If you are the only one conducting the interview, at least you will know and have the confidence that you have been both careful and thorough.

Answering the Candidate's Questions

In reaching milestones A and B described in chapters 2 and 3, you assembled a comprehensive package of information about the position and the corporate environment in which it will be performed. This is far more information than candidates normally receive about a prospective employer and should make them reasonably well informed. You will be covering the duties and responsibilities at a good level of detail during these interviews, and you will need to know how well they understand them. The other areas of information, included in the position description, should also be opened for questions.

The specific areas you will want to speak to are reporting structure, profit responsibility, location and travel requirements, and compensation.

Reporting Structure. Be sure the candidates understand who they would be working for and who would be working for them. This is an important aspect of any job and deserves comment. It could be a key attraction for the candidates.

Profit Responsibility. This too can be a powerful attraction to candidates for a management position. They will want to know if they indeed have the organizational and resource authority to control and influence the profits they would be responsible for. The degree to which control is vested in the position should be discussed.

Location and Travel Requirements. These can be real sticking points if they are not spelled out clearly. Candidates should know and agree to where they would be living, and approximately how much time away from home the job would normally require.

Compensation. Chapter 2 discussed the pros and cons of inserting the approximate salary in the position description. If it is included, candidates will already know what the salary and bonus arrangements are. If it is not included, now is the time to get it out on the table, so that he or she at least knows what the range is and what the bonus opportunities are. You will be extracting a good deal of past and present compensation information in the course of the first interview(s). If a person is clearly too expensive, you may as well admit it and go on to someone else. This is not the time to get into salary negotiations, but it is the time to face up to reality. Typically, when you go outside your own organization for an executive, you do not know exactly what you will have to pay for the talent you need. You only know what the salary range of the position is. As you talk to candidates you will learn what the marketplace has set in the way of compensation for the unique combination of skills and abilities you are seeking.

The fringe benefit package also deserves discussion. Much of this package is nontaxable and can help to offset a shortfall in direct compensation.

The company information should also be discussed at whatever level of detail the situation requires. At the least, the candidate should be asked if he has any questions about the information provided.

Confidential Disclosures

Usually, this is not the time for confidential disclosures. If you are recruiting a senior executive, however, to deal with a specific condition or set of problems—especially if the situation has received public attention—you may have difficulty getting into meaningful discussions until at least some sort of statement is made. Eventually you will have to get the problems out on the table and discuss them, warts and all. After all, you are looking for someone who will make a career commitment. It would be a gross deception not to give an executive the necessary information to make an informed choice.

You will have to make the decision as to when and how much information is divulged. At this point, however, you and the candidate are exploring needs and interests. As it appears that those needs can be met and interest increases, there will be time for fuller disclosure.

Assessing the Value of Industry Knowledge

Anyone you recruit to a management position will come to you from a different working environment, even if the company he or she leaves is a direct competitor. Industry knowledge and experience may be important and even critical to the successful performance of the individual and the company, so it is necessary to attempt to place an appropriate value on this aspect of the management employment process.

Companies which have attempted to diversify over the past ten years have sometimes found themselves in an industry or business activity so alien to their own that they could not operate effectively and profitably. The same thing can happen to people, but it would be unfair to the candidate and yourself as well to assume that it will happen. An intelligent and highly motivated person can acquire industry knowledge very quickly when offered the opportunity, and the transfer of methods and technology from another industry to your own may be the very reason you are employing a new manager.

It is beyond the purpose of this book to set forth guidelines on the importance and applicability of out-of-industry experience. Industry knowledge is more important in some areas of management than others, and perhaps less important at senior levels than middle-management levels. It is necessary to find out as much as you can through the interview about what candidates manage, how they manage, and the industry in which they do it.

Industry knowledge is never a substitute for management ability.

8
Predicting Job Performance
Milestone G

The evaluation of first interviews has been afforded milestone status on the Critical Path because it is at this point that the formal interviewing of candidates usually ends in the typical hiring process. If you were to stop at this point, get off the Critical Path, and make one of the candidates a job offer, you would be doing what most people do. And why not? After all, you have found one or more people who have the necessary knowledge, skills, abilities, education, and experience. You have satisfied yourself that he or she can do the job. Let's get on with it—check a few references and make the person an offer.

If you do that at this point, you will probably have done a more thorough job of evaluating the individual than you might have, had you not used the Critical Path Hiring method, but you will not be making as careful a selection as you could if you continued the process. You have determined if the individual can do the job—but will he? Most people who are unhappy or unsuccessful, or who fail in jobs, do not do so because they cannot perform, but rather because they won't perform. If you want to select the individual who has the best potential for success in the job, you will have to stay on the Critical Path, and now find out who will be the outstanding performer.

The people with whom you complete the first interview(s) will presumably be well worth your consideration. As you work your way through these interviews, you will be acquiring a perspective on a number of different areas relating to the hiring process. These include:

1. The effectiveness of the materials you have provided candidates to stimulate their interest and communicate the important things about the company and position

2. The relative abundance or scarcity of people in the job marketplace who appear to have the unique combination of attributes you are seeking

3. The adequacy of the compensation package you have attached to the position

4. The relatively small number of really qualified people there are for the position

Everyone will not rate a "10" in every important area of qualification. For this reason, it is necessary to complete the first interviews with all of the candidate–prospects you have assembled, deferring a judgment on any individual until all the scores are in. No one is either good or bad, except by comparison, and you may find that someone whom you thought had a serious weakness is, on second consideration, the best of the lot.

You may also find out that no one is suitably qualified, and you will have to make some adjustments in the job definition, the compensation, and/or the method you have chosen to attract candidates. Unfortunately, you cannot just add up each candidate's rating and base your choice on aggregate scores, for obvious reasons. You will have to consider the total candidate in the case of each person, and make a choice. By now there is a good deal of information available on each person in the candidate file. This is the time to review it. The people you select now for further consideration will be the group from which you ultimately hire the one best person. Hopefully, that group will consist of three or four viable candidates. Nobody likes a choice of one. If you do not have that many, make the adjustments referred to above.

The Forces at Work in the Selection Process

In the best of all possible worlds, you could now make a completely unbiased and objective choice—but such Solomon-like wisdom is hard to exercise where people are concerned. There are a number of factors to consider which are over and above what is in the candidate file. Some of these are:

1. The personality of the candidate—how you and the candidate relate to each other

2. The relative importance of industry knowledge and experience to the performance of the job

3. The personal chemistry between the candidate and others in the company or organization (a search committee for example) who may have participated in the first interviews

4. The need to objectively evaluate people from within your own organization who are being reviewed for the position along with those from outside

5. The need to give proper consideration, and even priority in some instances, to women and minorities

6. The need to control employment cost and ongoing salary costs

7. How urgent it is to fill the position as quickly as possible

The most relentless of these issues may be time, but such urgency keeps the hiring process moving ahead.

So with whom do you move ahead? Make that choice now by reviewing the information you have collected on each candidate.

Interpreting Educational Qualifications

The best educated person is not always the person with the best overall qualifications, or the best developed management skills. If a bachelor's degree from an accredited college is a minimum requirement, you may have to set aside a person who is otherwise a good prospective candidate. Do not be in too big a hurry to consign this person's application to the paper-shredder, however. You may need him or her later on.

A college education accompanied by a bachelor's or graduate degree is a tremendous asset to anyone. A degree is clear evidence that a person has completed a course of study. Unfortunately, it tells you little about the quality of the education received. It is possible to receive an excellent education and never complete a four-year course of study. That is why it is necessary to speak to the candidate about his or her college experience, and the non-collegiate educational experiences too.

Interpreting Work Experience

As stated repeatedly, the best evidence of future performance is past performance. But you have to understand the candidate's past work experience to evaluate it properly. Look it over now and make some decisions about the questionable or weak spots you detected in the interviews. Were the duties consistent with the accomplishments? Were the accomplishments recognized and rewarded by higher compensation and/or advancement? Sometimes people advance in companies in lock-step based on time in a position rather than demonstrated excellence. Do not overlook the importance of being in the right place at the right time either.

Was the person in the position long enough? To have had an impact and to have grown, a manager should have been in a position long enough to have gone through the all-important cycle of planning–implementing–evaluation–correction/fine-tuning. This is how experience is gained.

Did the candidate spend too much time in a position? A compelling argument can be made that unless the position changes significantly, the learning curve falls off rapidly after the first five years. We have all heard of the five-year veteran who has had one year of experience five times. Do not overvalue position tenure. More is not always better.

Interpreting the Candidate's Responses Concerning Duties and Responsibilities

Look over the ratings you have assigned to the candidates on the things they will be doing in the job on a day-to-day basis. Can you visualize them performing the tasks in your work environment? How effective will they be now versus a year from now? Will you or someone else in your organization be able to backstop and support them until the needed growth takes place? Will the growth take place? (You will learn something about that in the second interviews.) Or will you have to assign some duties and areas of responsibility permanently to someone else? And what effect will that have on someone else's performance? Asking and answering these questions as fully and honestly as possible will lead you to the correct selection of that handful of candidates you will want to proceed with.

The Other Things You Observed

It is impossible to conduct first interviews without collecting a number of reactions and impressions. They exist in your mind but they are, at this point, unorganized. In the second interviews, you will organize them and give them the importance to the overall evaluation they deserve.

For now, it is sufficient just to inventory those impressions for future reference. Ask yourself if the candidate was:

> Argumentative?
>
> Overly assertive?
>
> Attentive, a good listener?
>
> Confident?
>
> Alert?
>
> Articulate?
>
> Defensive or evasive?
>
> Indecisive?
>
> Candid?
>
> Accurate?
>
> Relaxed and at ease?

All of these are adjectives describing how candidates might have handled themselves in the interview—the image they might have projected. These traits can influence your assessment of a candidate, however, if you allow them to. Perhaps you should. If the candidate continually interrupted your questions, for example, to answer questions you did not ask, you might reasonably assume that it is a disturbing habit of that person which you neither want to live with nor try to change. On the other hand, it could be just a manifestation of the nervousness and stress the candidate is experiencing in interviewing for a position he or she wants badly. It would be better to wait for the second interviews, where you can explore why the candidate behaves in this manner, before reaching any final conclusions.

Where Do You Go from Here?

When you have made your selections, let the candidates know promptly and schedule the second interviews. Be just as prompt in letting candidates know when they have been eliminated from contention. That duty is sometimes overlooked, and it is decidedly unprofessional to let it happen. The candidate has gone to a good deal of time and trouble to answer your questions, and so deserves a direct answer.

Now let us get on with the really interesting part of Critical Path Hiring—predicting future performance.

9

The Second Interview(s)

Milestone H

Like the first interview discussed in chapter 7, the second interview may in fact be more than one session. It will be as many as you need to rate the candidate in nine personal qualities. The following building block qualities are "touchstones" in that they can be assembled into a performance-prediction profile. In the Critical Path Hiring process they are referred to as success factors:

Energy level

Goal orientation

Monetary motivation

Psychic reward needs

General ability

People skills

Adaptability/flexibility

Self-image

Management style

Measuring these qualities in the individual is of critical importance in CPH. The degree to which they are present in the candidate, and the degree to which they are required by the position, will determine in large part whether he or she will be happy, productive, and successful in the position, or unhappy, ineffective, and unrewarded.

Can you really predict future performance? Can you really tell from an interview how an individual will perform or behave on a day-to-day basis over an extended period of time? After all, candidates are on their best behavior in an interview. They certainly are not going to betray personal flaws if they can possibly help it. Nevertheless, the answer to these questions is yes, you can recognize winners with a high degree of accuracy if you know what to look for and how to read the signals. There is a limit to what you can hope to accomplish in the time you have to interview someone, but it is still possible to detect a great deal, and some of it will surprise you.

The Position Environment

In chapter 3, we talked about defining and describing the corporate environment as a tool in the recruiting process and as a means of educating the candidate in the values of the company. Now you must take a hard, objective look at the position itself, and make a careful estimate of how important each of the nine success factors is to the proper and acceptable performance of the management task.

Figure 9–1 provides a rating sheet which allows the scoring of each factor on a 0 to 10 scale. Before you rate the candidate in the success factors, you will first have to rate the job. When you have done that you will have profiled the position environment.

If you are thinking this isn't going to be easy, you are correct. That's right. There had to be a hooker somewhere. This is the hooker. You will have to take an honest look at the job, and maybe at yourself too (if the position reports to you) and perhaps ask yourself whether you will be able to give the person a pat on the back or other recognition when he or she has earned it—or whether you really want a strong leader in the position—or how strong a self-image the candidate has to have to stand up to the strong-willed peers he or she will be dealing with day to day.

You know your company and the real requirements of the position. If you don't set the minimum requirements in each of the success factors, you will only be shooting holes in the bottom of your boat. The water will flow in, not out. In the next chapter, we will talk about comparing the ratings of candidates to the position-environment profile.

None of the values you establish in this process should be below a 5. In a responsible management position, a 5 in any success factor

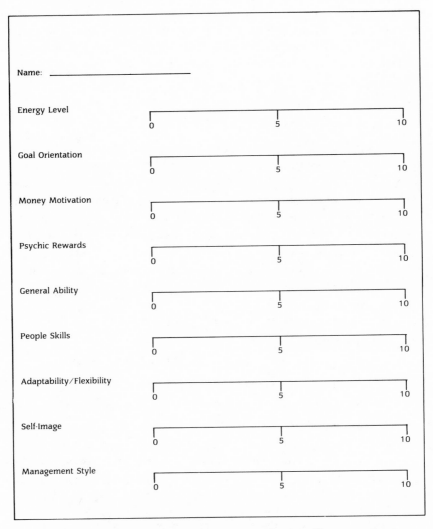

Figure 9–1. *Success Factor Rating Sheet*

is a minimum requirement. They can't all be 10's either. That would be unrealistic. Logically, the values you ascribe should be in the 5 to 7 range. They will establish the base-line level of acceptability for a candidate.

In using CPH, you would normally develop the position-environment profile as soon as the position definition described in chapter 2 is completed, long before you get into serious discussion with any candidate. The development of the environment assessment is properly a part of defining the position. It is included in this part of the text because of its dependence on a discussion of the success factors.

How the Success Factors Work

It is difficult in an interview situation to make judgments about an individual's leadership ability (or potential) in your job environment. Leadership ability is an abstract quality which does not lend itself to easy definition. So too are expressions like ambition, mental toughness, perceptiveness, or fire-in-the-belly. What you can do in the interview situation, however, is to look carefully at the degree to which the nine success factors are present in the candidate, and attempt to measure them. Leadership ability, for example, requires strength in the following areas:

> Energy—on a scale of 0 to 10, well above 5
>
> Goal orientation—also very high
>
> Psychic needs—should have an achievement need
>
> Communications skills (general ability)—very well developed
>
> People skills—warm and reasonably empathic
>
> Self-image—very positive

The candidate should also rate at least a "5" in the other success factors.

In CPH you do not have to make a decision on leadership ability while you are in the interview situation. You can rate the candidate in each of the nine success factors and then analyze them at your leisure.

How to Conduct the Second Interview

As with the first interview(s), you will have to control the flow of information. Unlike the first interview, where direct questioning is required, you will have to rely on indirect inquiries and careful observation to make the necessary evaluations. You will have to draw candidates out—get the people to talk about themselves—to find out what you need to know. If you were successful in obtaining the biographical sketch mentioned in chapter 5, it may provide some hooks to get you into discussions relating to the success factors. If not, approach the interview as though you are preparing a brief biography. Most people are willing to and enjoy talking about themselves if they think someone is interested. You are really interested.

Use the rating sheet shown in figure 9–1 to record your observations and assessments. The interview is over when you have recorded your estimate of the individual in each of the nine success factors.

Here are some do's and don'ts:

1. *Do* be interested in getting to know the candidate. If you are insincere, the candidate will sense it quickly. You have plenty of reason to be sincere.

2. *Do* take enough time to make a valid rating in every one of the nine factors. This cannot be done in fifteen or thirty minutes or maybe not even an hour. It may in fact take two or more interviews.

3. *Do* create a relaxed and private climate for this meeting. Do not allow the phone, your secretary, or anyone else to intrude. In this type of interview it is difficult to reestablish the dialog after an interruption.

4. *Don't* ask direct questions. You cannot learn about people's energy level by asking them how energetic they are. Ask questions which will stimulate the expression of attitudes, preferences, and opinions.

5. *Don't* discuss the job. The candidate will probably try to bring it up, which is only normal. Don't let it happen. You have already found out what you need to know in that area.

6. *Don't* get personal. You should steer the discussion away from personal disclosures. It is surprising how much of their private lives people will reveal if they think someone is interested. Cut it off if it is not needed to give you a handle on one of the nine factors.

Evaluating Women and Minorities

In the Lerner and Loewe musical *My Fair Lady*, Professor Henry Higgins laments, "Why can't a woman [Eliza Doolittle] be more like a man?" The answer, of course, is that if she were more like a man, she would not be Eliza Doolittle. Neither can a black be like a white, nor can members of a minority be expected to transform themselves into members of the majority. In doing so, he or she would lose his or her "persona"; that composite of characteristics that make up an individual personality. In fact, a woman does not have to behave like a man, nor does a black or other minority group member need to turn into a white to be an effective manager. The factors which determine how successful an individual will be in a management position have little to do with sex, race, or ethnic background. On the other hand, sex, race, and ethnic background may influence greatly an individual's life experience. Life experience, in turn, can influence some of the success factors.

Some of the lines of questioning suggested in association with the success factors may not be very reliable indicators where women or minorities are concerned. For example, you could be wrong in concluding that a woman was not overly energetic because as a child she did not seek out the same kinds of small jobs to earn pocket money, or to just be doing something, that a boy might have. She could have been specifically prevented from such activities by parents, peers, or society in general. The same applies to team sports, or anything else a parent, teacher, or authority figure felt was unladylike at the time. Attitudes about appropriate youth experience for women are changing, but there is little chance that they will ever be identical with those for men. They do not need to be. It may be an intellectual challenge, but you will have to take into consideration the differences in life experience that society dictates in evaluating some of the success factors.

The same caveat applies to blacks and other ethnic minorities. Their role models, societal influences, and life experiences also may be different from those of a white male. You must make an effort to get to know the candidate as a person in those areas of inquiry which bear on the success factors. This is a principal objective of the second interviews—making a personal acquaintance of the candidate. If you do this, you will be able to evaluate the individual in the context of your organization, and the candidate's ability to be successful will become more clear to you.

The best way to overcome stereotypical notions, which influence us all, is through knowledge of the person.

Management Skills versus Success Factors

Administrative, organization, and planning skills are learned or acquired abilities, gained through education and experience. They should not be confused with success factors, some of which may also be acquired through a learning experience, but on a less conscious level. Decisions about the level of an individual's managerial skills and abilities will normally be made in the first interviews. Decisions about an individual's propensity to improve or acquire new skills will be made in the second interviews.

It is appropriate to point out that many of the nine success factors are under the direct control of the individual, and if he wishes he can change them, either permanently through behavior modification or temporarily through a conscious effort on his or her part. For this reason indirect questioning and careful observation of not only *what* is said in response, but *how* it is said is necessary for a valid rating by you.

The point is that *he* can change these qualities, not *you*. The odds that you could change the candidate's behavior in any of the nine areas on any sort of permanent basis are almost nonexistent.

The Nine Factors

The concept of these nine factors (energy level, goal orientation, monetary motivation, psychic reward needs, general ability, people skills, adaptability/flexibility, self-image, and management style) has evolved over years of interviewing and executive evaluation experience. By limiting the areas of observation and judgment to nine qualities, the performance-prediction process becomes manageable and achievable.

Any management position (with the exception of those which require artistic ability) can be profiled in terms of the nine qualities.

The process of attaching a value to each factor, where an individual candidate is concerned, is of course judgmental on your part.

Energy Level

Given an acceptable level of other success factors in a candidate, energy level becomes critical in whether someone is a good performer, an excellent one, or an outstanding contributor. A lot has been said about working smart and not hard, but there is strong evidence that high achievers work both hard and smart, and that they do it continually throughout their careers.

Energy level is not an absolute value. It is only significant in comparing two or more people, or comparing one person to a representative group. A high energy level can't be artificially sustained for a long period of time, nor will it make up for large deficiencies in the other success factors, but where the other factors appear approximately equal, choose the candidate who has the highest energy.

How does one judge energy level in people? Here are some techniques which have been used successfully:

1. Ask about the earliest jobs they remember as a child. High energy often shows up early in life. Job activities outside the home at an early age indicate a drive to be doing something and earning money at it. Three or more jobs by age twelve, sometimes even simultaneously, is not uncommon.

2. Ask about sports activities in school and college, as well as after-school and summer work activities.

3. Find out what social and community activities people have taken part in, and how much they were involved in organizing and leading the activities.

4. Ask how candidates spend a typical work day, what time they get to work, when they organize the work, and how long they work on the average.

5. Manage during the interview to take a walk with the candidate. Let him or her set the pace. The vigor and pace with

which a person moves may contribute to your overall opinion of energy level.

These observations should give you an impression of relative energy levels between two or more people.

Goal Orientation

Sir Edmund Hillary is credited with saying, "Because it was there," in response to a reporter who asked him why he climbed Mt. Everest. Hillary's book, *High Adventure*, reveals that he derives a great deal of personal pleasure from testing the limits of his physical and mental ability.

All people, to some degree, are internally motivated to achieve goals. It is the degree to which some people structure their lives and focus their energies and attention on their goals that makes them more or less achievement-oriented than others. If they are able to communicate their enthusiasm for their goals to others, then they have one of the more important elements of leadership ability.

If a person is a marathon runner or a scratch golfer, it may tell you something about his or her athletic ability or ability to concentrate, but not necessarily about goal orientation, unless the person approaches other aspects of working and living with the same competitive spirit.

Goal orientation, like other success factors, is a relative value. Indirect questioning can provide some insights into the candidate's strength of commitment as well as ingenuity in achieving personal goals.

1. Inquire about how the individual has spent his or her time as a youth, and as an adult. In play? Work? What does he or she do for personal enjoyment?

2. Ask for a description of some achievements in personal and business life, and how the person structured his or her time and energy to accomplish those goals.

3. Inquire how the person goes about transmitting personal enthusiasm for work goals to the people he or she manages.

4. Ask about the individual's parents' attitudes toward achievement, work, and responsibility. Parental attitudes make strong and often lasting impressions on all of us.

Monetary Motivation

Today, people have two types of monetary goals: the income potential to meet their personal-compensation expectations and the income growth needed to offset the effect of inflation. Psychologists differ on whether and how much money in the form of wages motivates people. It would be unjust to attempt to discuss compensation theory in so short a space. The fact is that most senior management positions carry financial inducements to encourage high performance. It is worthwhile in selecting people for these positions to form an opinion about how well and how long these inducements may work for any given person.

Dollar expectations are worth exploring for a number of reasons. The salary and bonus which a position carries are viewed by some as a status symbol or a level of achievement in the corporate hierarchy. They are the means of supporting a life-style which may be very important to a person. They may be a necessity because of unique medical, education, or family needs. Also they are a means of security and independence in old age, and a hedge against the uncertainties of life.

Income-related indirect questioning in interviews may be particularly revealing in some areas.

The candidate's family life. What do they do together as a family? Travel? Sports? Inquire about children, including their educational plans and health needs.

Lifestyle. What does the candidate envision for family and self?

The candidate's own youth. Personal preferences regarding home and mode of living can be heavily influenced by a person's early experiences.

The individual's investment philosophy. Real Estate? Money market certificates? Stocks and bonds? Keen interest in these areas of investment and the ability to talk intelligently about them demonstrate knowledge of the uses of money.

Nonmonetary Job Expectations (Psychic Rewards)

There are a lot of reasons why people work. To earn an income is only one of them. One noted psychologist, Dr. Frederick Herzberg, believes that money only has the power to prevent job dissatisfaction, and that other factors related to work are the true motivators. Work fills psychic reward needs, and these may be more important to a candidate than direct compensation.

It would be impossible to list all the psychological rewards that work offers. A few examples may make the point, however.

A salesman is promoted to sales manager, but is unhappy and fails in the job because he loses the achievement reward of closing a sale. Participating vicariously in the sales success of the people he counsels and manages is not an adequate substitute.

A person is promoted from plant controller to company controller. She has been located in the headquarters building, but on promotion she is relocated to larger office space in a building ten miles from headquarters. Her performance deteriorates and she looks perpetually unhappy. The reason may be that she has lost her informal contact with the rest of the management team and her sense of belonging.

It is expensive in many ways to hire or promote people into high management positions and have them fail or not perform up to expectations because of a missing psychic reward.

Some people feel awkward or embarrassed in talking about the nonmonetary rewards of a position. The following questions may help you develop a feel for whether the individual is a good fit for the position in this respect.

1. What gave you the most and least satisfaction in the positions you've held in the past?

2. How do you feel about representing the company in trade associations, civic activities, and so forth?

3. What do you consider an ideal working environment for you personally?

4. Have your other employers encouraged frank and open discussions of company problems among management?

5. How much freedom for independent action do you think a manager should be allowed?

6. Do you think your other places of employment have been creative environments?

Questions such as these may provide insights into some of the individual's needs which must be met if the position is to be gratifying. You, as the manager, will know how realistic those expectations are. Base your rating on how well the person's psychic needs can be met in the position.

General Ability

If you, as a senior officer of a company, were to make the decision to only hire managers with IQs above 130, you would end up with a very intelligent management team. You might also end up with a disaster. Exceptional managers are a unique combination of many factors, above-average intelligence being only one of them.

Clearly, the best way to measure general ability is through controlled testing, but in any event some subjective judgments of candidates' general ability must be made if they are to be entrusted with critical control. What you may learn from talking with people may not help you much in measuring their ability to read and comprehend, their arithmetic and logical ability, or even their vocabulary. They may be just good conversationalists.

The right questions can provide some insights into an individual's level of ability in the areas just mentioned. Do not use trick questions, however. An interview is a stress situation, usually far in excess of normal job stress in a working environment. Responses to trick questions in this situation could be very misleading.

Try these straightforward queries:

1. What were your high school and college grade point averages?

2. What courses did you like and excel at?

3. Did you win any scholarship awards?

4. How many and what kinds of books do you read in a typical year?

5. Do the written responses provided by the candidate demonstrate well-developed writing skills and an ability to articulate feelings, attitudes and opinions?

Notice whether the candidate's oral responses during the interviews demonstrate clarity of thought, a good command of language, a grasp of the technical and administrative requirements of the position, and the ability to focus on a question.

People Skills

Conducting a business, or managing a department or division of a company, is more than a little like conducting a symphony. Those who are best at it know what is an acceptable level of performance, know what each person and group must deliver to make the performance a success, and perhaps most important, know how to invoke the best effort each person is capable of. To do this, the conductor has to have both personal commitment and leadership style.

Today's business management styles tend more and more toward a more empathic relationship between manager and employee, the purpose being to draw forth everyone's best efforts to achieve a virtuoso performance by the company. To get this, you have to know the best that each person is capable of, and to know this you have to know the person. The genius of the manager in a participative management system is to know each person's creative capability and how to encourage that capability without sacrificing control.

There is a wide range in managerial attitudes between the two extremes of *Theory X* and *Theory Y* which organizational behaviorist Douglas McGregor describes in his book, *The Human Side of Enterprise* (New York: McGraw-Hill, 1960). Just how much people-sense a manager will need to function effectively in the position in question will depend on where the department, division, or company stands along the continuum between points X and Y. The following questions may provide some insights:

1. How do you go about goal assignment in the group you manage? (Does the individual set goals *for* people or *with* people?)

2. Do you think the channels for upward communication work in your company? How would you improve them?

3. Do you think people work as diligently in a relaxed environment as in a highly regulated one?

4. Look for aloofness as contrasted to personal warmth. Does the individual speak easily and frequently? Is he or she relaxed in your presence? Does the candidate demonstrate rigidity and coldness in business dealings?

5. Does the individual show sensitivity and awareness of how others are reacting to him or her?

Flexibility/Adaptability

It seems that every business magazine and newspaper periodically carries an article approximately entitled "How to Cope with the Decade of the 80s." First they talked about new management methods. Then it was new products, new materials, new processes, new employee relations, new methods of distribution, and new methods of accounting, capital development, and finance. The substance of these articles is that the companies that will be around at the end of the 80s are those which are alert to change and can respond quickly.

Flexibility and adaptability to a changing business environment is difficult to establish and maintain in a management team. The reason is that change involves a measure of risk-taking. By definition, trying something new means departing from the known and venturing into the unknown. It requires a willingness and ability on the part of a manager to plan, implement, analyze, evaluate, and respond quickly. It is hard work. But this hard work makes the difference between risk-taking and gambling.

Like other success factors, the qualities of flexibility and adaptability—the will to try new things and to take thoughtful, reasonable risks—are not easy to measure in an individual in a short span of time. The following observations and lines of questioning may be helpful:

1. How do you stay on top of new developments in your field?

2. Do you attend professional group meetings? Trade shows and conferences?

3. Tell me about a significant change in your operation (area of responsibility) which you spearheaded.

4. How often do you take a critical look at competitive products and alternative methods?

5. If you had the time, would you go back to college for a refresher course?

6. How do you go about stimulating interest in and selling new ideas within your present company?

Self-image

We have known short people who stand tall and tall people who stand short (or try to); assertive people, and shy, retiring people; people who dominate or try to dominate others; people who look you straight in the eye, and those who won't. "Laid-back," "sincere," "mature," "pugnacious," "insecure," "abrupt," and dozens of other adjectives are used to describe the images that individuals project.

Some self-images, as might be shown by a rich, commanding voice, are carefully cultivated, with a fine sensitivity for their impact on the other person. Others are completely unstructured. Some images are very positive, and others are downright devastating in how they affect other people. We have known people who were very courteous, polite, and pleasant to their peers and those above them in the organization. Some of those people, however, were rude and abusive to those below them. So genuineness also comes into consideration.

In interviewing, you will become aware of small things about people which can contribute to the image of themselves which they are projecting to you, intentionally or otherwise. In the preceding chapter, you inventoried some of those images from the first interviews; confirm or discard them now. If the individual slouches in the chair, has fluttering hands, does not listen intently when you are speaking, or does any one of a thousand little things which may turn you off personally, it may influence you one way or another about that person's overall qualifications and ability to contribute. But try to be as objective as possible. Some of these little aberrations may be no more than that, mere deviations from the norm due to the stress of the situation.

You have to be the judge of whether the self-image individuals project would help or hurt them in the position. Self-image is more important in some positions than in others. There are no questions you can ask which will give you a reliable reading of this quality. You just have to observe and note.

Management Style

We all know situations in which an executive is employed to fill a key management position and then does not live up to expectation. On the face of it, the person is well qualified by reason of education, experience, motivation, and overall ability. The symptoms may be "lacks people skills," "fails to delegate," "wouldn't take initiative," or "did not develop his or her people." The underlying reason may be a conflict of management systems between old and new employers.

Colleges and universities today teach that there are essentially four different management systems in operation in American business. These are: participative group, consultative, benevolent-authoritative, and exploitive-authoritative. Our purpose here is not to define the characteristics of these systems, but rather to point out that they exist and that they influence the management styles of the executives who work within the systems. The transition from one system to another may not be easy, and sometimes not possible at all for a given manager. This is because their concept of the source of their management authority and prerogatives may be deeply rooted in their personalities and past work experiences.

If individuals are to be good fits with your organization, they will either have to have had experience with your management style, or be sufficiently adaptable to change. It is appropriate to mention also that differing management systems can exist side by side in divisions or departments of the same company. It is a good idea to give consideration to how the former manager ran the department when seeking his or her replacement.

The following questions may provide a clue to what individuals perceive the source of their management authority to be:

1. How widely do you think decision-making authority and accountability should be distributed in an organization?

2. Describe how you personally make a management decision.

3. Do you believe frank and open discussion of problems in your area of responsibility is a good idea?

4. Do you prefer for people to come to you with problems or answers?

5. Are you satisfied with your second-line management people?

If some of the suggested lines of questioning make you uncomfortable, then do not use them. You will have to find other ways to make the assessments. Either way, they will have to be made. The stakes are too high to do otherwise.

All of the success factors described in this chapter *do* bear directly on the ability of the candidate to be successful in the position. The problem in assessing these factors is not with the factors themselves, but rather with the tools at the disposal of working managers by which these assessments can be made. Managers have only one tool, really, and that is the ability to ask questions and interpret the responses. Fortunately, most candidates for executive positions understand the necessity for care in management employment. They have been there and are willing to cooperate.

10
Predicting Job Success
Milestone J

Previous chapters cautioned against establishing premature preferences for one candidate over another. Admittedly, this is difficult to avoid. By now you have held several meetings with one or more individuals, and you have explored virtually every aspect of the position with them. In the second interviews you focused exclusively on the success factors, examining them with a surgeon's skill. It is only natural that by now you would begin to establish a preference. Try to defer this just a little longer.

One of the collateral benefits of Critical Path Hiring is that the procedure brings the prospective employer together with the candidate for a number of meetings. Each of these meetings should be more comfortable than the previous one and the stress is relieved for both participants. Some of those evidences of nervousness are gone now and you see candidates as they really are. First impressions are tempered by knowledge and familiarity.

Another advantage is that candidates have a thorough understanding of the position and what would be expected of them, as well as knowledge of the company and insights into the attitudes of management. They have been learning too. Most important, they know they are being carefully considered and that they have had the opportunity to present themselves in the most effective manner.

You now have enough information to make some accurate predictions about how successful your candidates will be in the position. It is time to organize and interpret what you have learned.

Rating Values

It would be wonderful if you could now just add up the values you have ascribed to each candidate in the nine success factors, take the aggregate score to a table, and derive the success probability from it. Wonderful—but not very realistic. A candidate could be woefully lacking in one or two factors, but sufficiently strong in others to make the total score impressive. Also, not all management positions require high values in all of the factors.

In all probability, what you will have done in assigning rating values is subconsciously use yourself as the norm. Is the candidate as energetic, goal-oriented, and money-motivated as I am? If you assign a value of 5 to yourself in each category, then the scores for each factor begin to take on meaning. There is nothing wrong with constructing the value method this way. There has to be some frame of reference. On a practical level, however, assuming you are a senior executive, you will probably have more than average strength in each of the nine success factors. The result could be unrealistic expectations as to how well a candidate should score to be acceptable to you. But there is a way out of the dilemma of using yourself as the norm. It is to develop a broader frame of reference. If you form the habit of viewing everyone you come in contact with, not just other managers but everyone, in terms of the nine success factors, you will quickly develop a broader perspective on these values. Not coincidentally, you will begin to make some fascinating and accurate observations of how people are going to act and react. There is another advantage to broadening your frame of reference—it is almost impossible to attach a dispassionate and objective value to yourself in each of the nine factors.

The Value of Arithmetic

Even if aggregate scores do not tell you all you need to know, they still tell you something. If the candidate rated a 5 in each factor, the total score would be 45. The standard distribution curve in the introduction to this book indicates that a score of 45 is the midpoint. An average performer.

Everything in the Critical Path Hiring method is directed toward the selection of candidates who are on the forward side of the performance curve. No matter how well qualified candidates may appear to be in terms of industry knowledge, skills, abilities, education, and experience, if they are not in the 45 to 90 range, with at least a 5 in each factor, they will be average or poor performers in the position. If you do not believe this, take the time right now to develop a performance index for each member of your present management team. It is easy enough to do. You know them and work with them daily. Rate each of them on the success factors, and chart them on the rating sheet shown in figure 9–1. Now, how well does the overall performance of each individual, as you have observed it, correlate with the ratings you have established? Interesting, isn't it?

Catalysts

The success factors can be viewed as catalysts, those mystical ingredients that make things happen. Consider some of the terms, adjectives, and phrases that are often used to describe effective and successful executives, as shown in table 10–1.

You may not agree with this hypothesis of what makes a decisive person. It is statements like these which make for endless debate. What is really important is not that you agree or disagree, but that you try to make an objective judgment about the degree to which a success factor is present in the individual you are interviewing. You will learn by observation and retrospection whether you defined the term correctly. The more you discipline yourself to look at people in terms of the success factors, the more accurate your assessment of these factors will become.

Do-It-Yourself Psychology

There is a point of diminishing returns in attempting to judge using our success factors. When you have thought about an individual for fifteen or twenty minutes in these terms, you have probably reached that point. There is a lot more to human behavior than can be explained by success factors. Their purpose is only to provide you with glimpses into the persona of the individual behind the mask. If these glimpses give you some cause for concern, or if you simply want to know more, it is time to turn the matter over to a professional. Either

Table 10–1
Table of Success Factor Equivalents

Term (Quality)	Catalyst(s)
Leadership	High energy, well-defined goals, achievement need, communication ability, people-sense, positive self-image
Mental-toughness	Well-defined goals, people-sense, strong self-image, little need for approval
Decisiveness	Achievement need, adaptability/flexibility, positive self-image
Management ability	Well-defined goals, people-development need, communications ability, people-sense, adaptability/flexibility, positive self-image
Tenacity	Strong goal orientation, strong achievement need
Dedication/commitment	High empathy for people, approval and achievement needs, good communications skills

an industrial psychologist or a psychiatrist can give you an expert opinion. It is time well spent to get to know your psychologist, however, if you really want to understand what he or she is saying to you.

At this point, you may be asking yourself if you really want to play psychologist in the management hiring process. It is true that you can dispense with a good deal of this burden if you routinely rely on an outside professional to check your choices—but fewer than 1 percent of all management selections are ratified this way. The fact is, in making your choices you are usually going to rely on your own observations, and perhaps those of a few others in your own organization.

Personal Chemistry

Now is the time to consider personal chemistry, comfort level, personality, fit, or whatever you choose to call your gut feelings about the other person as a human being. By considering personal chemistry now, rather than early in the selection process, you are limiting your thinking to those candidates who not only can do the job but also will be successful in it, if employed. It is a "safe-safe" situation now, and you can allow your subconscious to take over for a little while.

Unfortunately all of the success factors do not add up to a pleasing personality. Earlier we pointed out that you are not hiring a golf partner, but if you are really more comfortable with one candidate than another at this point, do not ignore it any longer.

The Impact of Appearance

Various studies purport to show that physically attractive people are more likely to be employed than unattractive ones; that tall men are more likely to be hired to management positions than short men; and that very feminine-appearing women are at a disadvantage with their less feminine-appearing sisters in advancing in a business environment. In CPH, we are advocating an executive-hiring methodology which will yield a lot better reasons for hiring or not hiring a person than such shibboleths as these. Physical characteristics have virtually nothing to do with ability, yet they unreasonably influence the unwary person. Do not allow it to happen—be wary of your own tendencies in this regard.

A person's clothes can tell you something about personality. There can be no doubt that it is possible for an individual to dress for success. An executive should be expected to demonstrate at least a reasonable amount of clothes sense. If candidates for an executive position present themselves for consideration in modes of attire that are clearly out of keeping with customary business dress, you would have the right to ask yourself what sort of statement they are trying to make. Little confrontations such as these are not uncommon. You are being tested. If you allow them to pass uncontested, you may be leaving yourself open to larger confrontations down the road.

If you have an unofficial uniform in your company—and most businesses do—why not let people know it?

Personality and Perversity

There is little you can do in the interview situation to learn about whether an individual is pleasant or unpleasant to work with on a day-to-day basis. Anyone who has poor interpersonal habits will surely try to keep them hidden when interviewing. Daily life is made less than pleasant for tens of thousands of subordinates by managers who are rude and abusive, or guilty of sexual harassment. Other managers simply cannot leave their personal problems at home. There is no place for such behavior in a place of business. You may be able to gain some insights into this area of concern in the reference-checking process. It is worth your best efforts to do so.

Ego Management

Upper-level executives don't really have egos to feed, do they? No. Of course not. They are too busy dealing with everyone else's egos to develop their own. Still, just in case you run into an egoistic candidate, it is probably appropriate to comment on the subject.

If the job candidates you are interviewing have large egos, you will have discovered it long before now, especially if you have asked them to submit to the procedures described in this book. Most people with well-developed egos will have difficulty adjusting to the disciplines that CPH suggests. A real ego would be in tatters after going through the CPH process. Don't confuse ego with a positive self-image. The former can give you headaches; the latter is to be much esteemed.

In the context of CPH, there are telltale signs of egocentricity:

1. People may not want to comply with the CPH procedure, especially the provision of detailed information the forms request. They will usually plead lack of time or interest. If it really is lack of interest, you'll have to build that interest, if you can. You may want to capture the chronology of work and education plus the brief biography in an exploratory meeting, as suggested in chapter 6, if they really are too busy. If they aren't really too busy, they have already scored a point on you. It may well be that such individuals are top performers in your industry, so it is worthwhile to be a little accommodating at this point. You'll have to be the judge of that.

2. They will let you know quickly about all the little goodies their present company lavishes on them: a Mercedes, membership in several private clubs, access to a ski lodge in the Rockies and a beach house at Sanibel, and time off for the Mackinac races or the U.S. Open. The list isn't limited to items outside the office. It could include an office done in nineteenth century antiques with a sterling silver coffee service and bone china. You will have to find out if these applicants are worth so much.

3. Such people aren't necessarily going to be very helpful in the process of making those judgments either. They might be visibly nettled at the depth of questioning involved in CPH, and averse to the structured discussions which are taking place. They may also try to take control of the process and tell you what they think you need to know. Conversely, they may want to ride on their reputation in the industry and be noncommittal to you.

The scenario is clear. If the candidates really are heavyweights, you may want to pay the price. But the bottom line says they had better be able to deliver—on budget and on schedule.

Egos sometimes make humorous cocktail party talk, but they are hell to live with. Notwithstanding, every little executive perk is not necessarily a salve for the ego. There are times and situations when an ego-gratifying bonus could be justified on the basis of its worth to the company. If it enhances the productivity or effectiveness of the individual's work, and is cost justifiable, it doesn't qualify as an ego trip. The truth is, these little job enhancements may have been won as a result of hard work and significant accomplishment. If so, these "merit badges" may be hard to part with and may become bargaining chips in the compensation negotiations to follow. This is a good time to let candidates know what the company does and doesn't do in this regard—before they become sticking points.

11

The Hiring Decision

Milestone K

The first ten chapters of this book detailed a careful and deliberate procedure for executive evaluation and selection. Careful and deliberate does not mean slow, however. The entire Critical Path process can be executed in sixty days or less, depending on the number of candidates involved, and the time you commit to the task.

Now the process accelerates. You've found out everything you can hope to learn by talking directly to the candidates and, if you've followed the CPH process, you have plenty of information on which to decide with whom to proceed. This and the following two chapters discuss three crucial steps in the process:

Making the choice

Checking references

Negotiating the deal

These steps cannot be done in parallel. It is possible and recommended that the earlier steps in the CPH process be carried on with several candidates concurrently, for the sake of expediency. From here on you will have to treat each candidate serially, and quickly, to a final conclusion.

The Candidate Information File

When we left the candidate information file in chapter 6, it contained only a few items. Now, the file includes the following:

1. Initial candidate source and contact information

2. The brief biographical sketch prepared by the candidate

3. The chronology of education and work experience which the candidate prepared before the inception of discussions

4. The candidate's written comments on the duties of the position

5. Notes on all meetings with the candidate

6. Your ratings and others' ratings of the candidate on each duty

7. Your ratings of the candidate on the nine success factors, with others' ratings as well

8. Copies of all correspondence

This is a lot of data on one person, but it is organized and focused on the individual's ability to do the job and the personal qualities he or she can bring to the position. The fact that the data is organized makes it easy to analyze and interpret in forming an accurate decision. Now we describe the steps in the process of interpreting the information.

It's Meeting Time

If more than one person is involved in the hiring process, the time comes when differing viewpoints must be reconciled. This is the time. Especially in large companies, searches are frequently conducted by a committee. If everyone on the committee has been following the Critical Path Method, the stage should be set for some spirited discussion. On the other hand, if some members have not exercised due diligence, they cannot participate fully and objectively in the evaluation process. It would be difficult to overemphasize the importance of laying down the ground rules for the conduct of the search, at the beginning, among all interested parties.

The purpose of this meeting is to prioritize the qualified candidates so that you can enter into further discussions, negotiate an acceptable job offer, and consummate the hiring of one individual. To repeat, you cannot carry on this process simultaneously with two or more candidates. You must single out one with whom to proceed.

The Importance of Expedience

There is a compelling reason why the search committee must reach agreement quickly at this point. Up to now, presumably you have been carrying on dialogs with two or more individuals who are qualified, want the job, and would be successful if hired. You have to choose one with whom to proceed. But, if negotiations with that one are unsuccessful, you will want to proceed with the others. To preserve those options, you will have to move quickly or you will lose your candidates. What the process looks like to the candidates is this: they have been introduced to the company in a thorough and positive way by the information on the job and company provided them. They have responded properly to the information requests of milestone D. They have had several lengthy interviews with perhaps a number of people, who were well informed about them and the job and asked the right questions of them. Their interest has grown throughout this process to the point where they have provided references and other assurances. *They now want to talk job offer.*

If you do not maintain their interest at this point, you will lose them. They will begin to build defenses against rejection. They will start thinking of why they should not take the job, rather than why they should. Changing companies, managers, products, problems, production facilities, cities, schools, homes, and friends—all of these considerations will turn into negatives.

You have three to four weeks at most. Maybe less. Do not waste it.

The Evaluation Process

The evaluation process can be broken down into three steps.

1. Compare your ratings of the candidates on the duties of the job with their own self-evaluations. You will have to decide whether they have enough ability to do the job, where their weaknesses are, and whether they can be supported in the weak areas by you or others until they can develop in the position.

2. Judge whether they *will* do the job and develop in the position. Consider the candidates in terms of the nine success factors.

As mentioned earlier, some success factors are more or less under the control of the candidates. If they choose to, they can alter their behavior to project more or less of any of these qualities. A permanent alteration, however, in one or more of these qualities is unusual. By the time people are out in the work place and have had a job or two, their behavior patterns are pretty well set. If they are sufficiently motivated, they may be able to change some of these patterns to some degree, but *you* will not be able to change their patterns for them. What you see is what you get.

3. Correlate the information to be sure that there are no gaps in the candidates' work experience and that what you've been told is consistent with what they have told the other interviewers. If there are discrepancies, check them out before you hire.

More on Discrimination

Without exception, this book has concentrated on the dialog between employer and prospective employee and the evaluation of people in the context of specific job requirements. Nowhere has a distinction been drawn between male and female, black and white, or a handicapped person versus a more fortunate one. There is no distinction. If you follow the Critical Path outlined here, you will evaluate each person on the basis of what he or she can bring to the position and the company, and all the parties involved in the process will know it. Many people do not want preferential treatment in the hiring process. They do want to believe that they have been carefully and thoroughly considered and that they have had the opportunity to put their best foot forward in an open and unprejudiced forum. If you provide that forum, you will have a high probability of hiring the right person for the job.

Special mention should be made of a particular group of potential employees—men and women over age forty. The average age in the United States has passed thirty and is rising. Additionally, the Social Security eligibility age has been raised to sixty-seven for those people born after 1960. As the population ages, more and more people will fall into the over-forty age group. Here are some worth-while observations on people in this age group, based on the author's years of management search work:

1. They have more experience than those under forty, and thus have had more time to sharpen their management skills.

2. They can bring maturity and cool judgment to your operations.

3. They can be an especially committed group in terms of dedication to their employer.

4. They are more likely to arrive early, work hard, and leave late than people junior to them.

5. They are in better health, and have more energy and vitality than their age group has previously enjoyed in the history of mankind.

In other words, it is not only illegal but also foolish to discriminate on the basis of age. You are trying to predict performance. The best evidence of future performance is past performance. It is easier to predict the performance of those over forty because there is more information on which to base the prediction.

Specialized Industry Knowledge

In chapter 7, industry understanding was commented upon. It bears repeating because the notion that industry knowledge will make up for lack of ability or shortfalls in the success factors is a snare and a delusion. Industry knowledge ranges in importance from very little to very much depending on the position you seek to fill. It is much more important in sales than in manufacturing or finance, for ex-ample. Industry knowledge can be rapidly acquired by an in-telligent, highly motivated manager. It happens every day. Manage-ment skills, on the other hand, are more slowly acquired, and some people never develop as skilled managers, no matter how much in-dustry knowledge they possess.

Given a choice between a person with broad industry know-how and poor management skills on the one hand and a skilled manager with limited industry knowledge on the other, opt for the skilled manager in a participatory management system. The odds are better.

One Candidate—or Three?

Throughout this book, I have stressed repeatedly the desirability of removing emotion from the executive hiring process. A case could be made that the author is obsessed with objectivity—and it would largely be true. Hiring on the basis of gut-level reaction or personal chemistry, because there is little else to go on—rather than on the basis of the disciplined evaluation procedure of CPH—is the single greatest trap in executive employment.

Working with someone with whom you have a personal empathy is certainly enjoyable. But, if the individual is only doing an average job, you may be paying a high price for companionship. It can also be highly enjoyable—and rewarding—to work with a professional who is a super-achiever, even if this star prefers antiquing or fly-tying to your favorite pastimes of racquetball and golf. An earlier chapter pointed out the multiple dependencies of the stockholders, customers, employees, and community. Those needs transcend all others.

Strategic Moves

Something is going to happen very quickly now between you and the final candidates, and you will have to be on your guard against it. The finalists will now sense very quickly that they are in fact finalists and that their bargaining position has improved markedly. They are, after all, exceptionally capable people. Just make sure you don't get carried away by one person's appeal. It would be a serious strategic error at this point to hold just one ace and discard the other two. You are heading into salary negotiations with the leading candidate, and your position will be stronger if you know you have more than one option which you can exercise with confidence. The way to avoid this risk is to keep a fallback candidate to begin negotiating with immediately if you can't come to comfortable terms with your number-one choice.

Further Discussions

You have now selected one individual with whom to proceed. You have called him or her into your office. There are two items on the agenda:

1. A disclosure of specific, perhaps confidential information which the candidate will need to make an informed job decision.

2. A request for the candidate's business references and permission to conduct a personal background check. Actually, you may want to obtain this information much earlier in the process. You can do it as soon as you've narrowed your choices to a manageable number.

Disclosures

Up to this point you have carefully controlled the flow of information between you and the candidates. Hopefully you have answered their questions politely and thoroughly. But you see, they may not know the right questions. It is time to tell them about the outbreak of leprosy in the mailroom, the controller's guilty secret, and the water in the basement. There is always a question about how much detailed information about the company's operations and problems should be revealed to an outsider. There are no hard and fast rules on this point. You will have to use your own judgment, based on the level of the position and how that confidential information may impact the candidate's attitude toward the job.

This much is clear: when people have not been told about the skeleton in the closet, the "real" reason why they are being hired, they generally tend to feel badly used and they begin to mistrust everything they are told. In the case of a CEO, or the head of a department, division, or major operating unit, it is inexcusable not to provide the best information available about current operating problems at this point. You may have a considerable amount of money at stake, but he or she has a career at stake. "Besides, if the person discovers the dirty linen only after taking the job, he or she may quit, sending you back to point zero." Candor at this point is the order of the day.

The Matter of the Spouse

The location of this discussion toward the rear of the book is not a reflection of the relative importance of the spouse in the recruitment of an executive. Chapter 2 pointed out that if the company expects the spouse to participate in company activities in any significant way, it should be indicated in the position description. Where recruiting an executive will involve the relocation of the person's family to the job site, you have the seeds of a dilemma.

Women's Changing Roles

Several reasons for the potential dilemma revolve around the changing roles of women in the workplace and the home. In the not too distant past the term *spouse* referred to the wife, who was supposed to be tractable, or at least give the appearance of being so, where relocations were concerned. Many wives are still cooperative where their husband's careers are concerned, but more and more they are asking hard questions which must be dealt with. Many now have active careers outside the home which would be impacted by a move to another city. Additionally, today the spouse we are talking about may be a man, not a woman.

To the extent that work activity or community attachment is psychologically rewarding to the spouse, and/or contributes importantly to the total family income, it will be a factor in the candidates' employment decision. If he or she does not bring the following considerations into the discussion, you may have to. Don't depend on the candidates to do so. It may be difficult for them to deal with constraints on their mobility, and they may put off a decision on moving until the last minute—only to find that the spouse has them up against a stone wall. There is more than one case of an individual who accepted a new job in another city and a year later was still trying to get the wife or husband to come along too.

Clarify the following issues with the surviving candidates no later than the end of the second interviews:

General Attitudes. How does the spouse feel about the move, if one is involved? Has the new position been discussed in depth with the spouse? Is the spouse familiar with the new location and its cultural advantages, recreational facilities, climate, cost of living, educational resources, and general quality of life?

Spouse's Employment. Is the spouse currently employed? Will he or she seek employment in the new location? How soon? At what compensation level? Some companies provide employment for the spouse also, if that person has a skill which can be utilized. Others may lend assistance (usually through the personnel department) in finding the spouse employment outside the company.

Specialized Educational or Medical Needs. It may be necessary to identify the location and scope of resources in the community to assure the spouse (and candidate as well) that these requirements can be met.

Real Estate and Lifestyle Requirements. If the candidate's family now owns three acres and stables two horses, you'll have to be the judge of whether the horses can be accommodated. If they are blue water sailors or downhill skiers, the presence or absence of nearby recreational facilities can be a factor in whether the individual (or family) will accept the position, once offered.

Family ties and the pull of the land can be factors in the employment decision. People who are native to Illinois may love the prairie, just as New Englanders may feel a special attachment to the White Mountains and snow. It isn't the climate. It's a deep-rooted kinship. Some uprooted people make the change easily, and for others it is incredibly painful. Sometimes key people resign a new position to move back home because they or their spouses are unhappy. You can't be absolutely certain that this won't happen, but you might want to at least discuss the possibility that it could occur.

Arranging the Wife's Visit

All of your efforts thus far to sell the job, the company, and the community have been focused on the candidate. Now it is time to lavish some attention on his or her spouse. The assumption for the purpose of this discussion is that the spouse is a wife, and that she has an important say in whether the candidate will accept the position. If you really want the individual, please read the rest of this chapter carefully. The spouse is pivotal! The candidate may not be able to function effectively without a domestic partner's support and assistance.

If you are recruiting a senior executive, someone in the $100,000-and-up category, odds are that his wife has already accepted the premise that the family's best interests will be served by her cooperation in any job change which appears to offer more money and career enhancement. Beware! This woman may well be the candidate's career manager. In any event, treat her as such. As for executives below $100,000 in compensation, the same caveat applies, with the added one that she may have a career of her own which has to be dealt with. The lines of inquiry just mentioned should provide some clues to where the wife's interests and concerns are. These should be dealt with on the wife's visit.

An information package providing a balanced overview of the community should be placed in the wife's hands prior to her visit. A good deal of this information is probably available from the Chamber of Commerce, but you may have to augment it with specific additional information which addresses some unique needs and interests. A suggested itinerary of her visit should also be prepared and reviewed with the candidate for suitability.

Who should host the wife's visit is a delicate point. Usually this task is relegated to the wife of one of the company executives. Some women seem to have an innate ability to put other women at ease. Others do not. You want to be sure the former kind is your hostess. If the visiting wife should end up feeling she is there to be evaluated and approved of, you may be in a lot of trouble. The age of the candidate's wife may be a factor also in the choice of a hostess; certainly her ability to be friendly, helpful, and diplomatic are crucial. Above all, she should be able to resist the temptation to share company gossip. The visitor does not have a frame of reference for evaluating such information and may be prejudiced by it.

Once the hostess is selected, she should be thoroughly briefed on how to handle the situation. Essentially, her mission will be to present the community in a positive, up-beat manner; to answer specific questions regarding concerns, needs, and interests; and to make the candidate's wife comfortable and welcome in the new surroundings. What she should not attempt to do is sell the candidate's wife on the job; discuss company problems; or probe the wife about personal matters or the candidate's interest in the job. These areas are a potential mine field. What neither you nor your hostess will know is how much the candidate may have disclosed to his wife about the company, the job, or his interest in the position in question. After the visit, the hostess should be thoroughly debriefed. She will undoubtedly have gained new information and insights.

Should you go through this procedure with the wife of each leading candidate? The answer depends on the candidate himself and also on how you elect to proceed, following the second interviews.

The wife can either make a deal or break a deal. If her impressions and reactions are positive, it could be the clincher that makes the negotiations with the candidate easier.

12
References and Background Checking
Milestone L

No matter how long you talk to individuals, or how good a rapport you establish, there are some things they are *not* going to tell you. Hardly a day goes by that someone in public or corporate life does not expose himself or herself (sometimes literally) to public criticism and/or ridicule and embarrassment. The media love these juicy little tidbits, although they are as much at risk as anyone of turning up with egg on their faces. When such a disclosure occurs, it reflects poorly on the individual and his or her employer as well. After all, what firm in its right mind would hire someone masquerading as a civil engineer to design a bridge on a public highway, someone with a phony medical degree to perform operations in the local hospital, or someone with a record of child molestation to run a day care center? These are only a few of the more sensational examples of careless employment practice.

On a less sensational level, you will want to know if candidates you are considering for a key executive position have lied to you about past positions they have held, why they left their previous employers, and what their educational credentials really are or are not. Or, whether they have any of a thousand patterns of behavior which may reflect poorly on your company, or cast doubt on the individual's ability to do the job.

The purpose here is not to describe what is good or bad, but only to urge you to find out all you reasonably can before you hire the person. It is far better to know in advance, and to then make a conscious decision about the matter, than to find out later to your embarrassment and regret. If such oversights happened only occasionally it would be less of a cause for concern. But, it happens with regularity, and most of it can be avoided. You may not care that your candidate, like Caesar's wife, be totally above suspicion. If you do care, however, here are some techniques to assist you.

Background Information Sources

What precisely constitutes a thorough background check can vary. What is acceptable under one set of circumstances might be superficial in another. At a minimum, do the following:

1. Verify past employment if possible, either by letter or telephone.

2. Verify academic credentials by contacting the college, university, or degree- or certificate-granting institution, either by letter or telephone.

3. Obtain a credit check of the individual through his or her local retail credit bureau.

4. Contact and discuss the individual with at least four business references whose names have been provided by the candidate.

A more thorough discussion of each of these reference sources is provided later in this chapter.

You will have to obtain releases from the candidate to conduct these checks, and some of the releases may have to be notarized. The application for employment will usually include a release for a check of previous employment if the application is properly worded and the candidate signs the form. Other background information sources you may wish to check include:

Local and state police
Private investigator services

Verification of Past Employment

In almost any major metropolitan area in the United States, it is possible to obtain a falsified driver's license and supporting Social Security card for under $200. If you are willing to spend $500 more, you can also obtain a college diploma and a record of past employment. Of course, these documents won't stand up under close scrutiny, but if they are accepted at face value by a prospective employer without verification, they are worth many times their cost.

No matter how comfortable you may be that the candidate is telling you the truth, you should still verify his or her record of past employment. In some cases, it may not be possible because a company has gone out of business, or been acquired or merged, so personnel records are no longer available. Where this occurs it is worth your best effort to talk to a business reference who can vouch for that segment of employment.

Unfortunately, about all you can expect from these checks is confirmation that the person was in fact employed there, the dates employed, and perhaps the position held. Privacy laws and the fear of legal action prevent most companies from formally commenting on reason for termination of employment, compensation, or job performance. You will have to get this information some other way.

Dates of employment should be double-checked. Compare what the candidate has told you and what other sources reveal. Look for gaps of more than a few months and question the candidate about them. You may find that there was a job in between that he or she didn't tell you about.

Verification of Academic Records

As has been indicated elsewhere in this book, the mere presence of a college degree or degrees is no assurance that the candidate is competent to do the job. However, if candidates state that they have degrees, and in fact do not—that is important. It calls to question everything else they may have told you.

In every profession and occupation requiring certification there are people in practice with falsified or nonexistent diplomas or licenses. It is so widespread as to be funny, unless of course one of these people is removing your appendix.

It is easy to verify that a diploma has been conferred by writing or telephoning the registrar or records office of the college or university in question. This information is normally provided without question by most institutions. If, however, you want grade transcripts or other detailed information, you will, because of privacy laws, have to obtain written permission from the candidate in a form acceptable to the institution. You may also have to wait awhile.

Confirmation from the source is preferable to a candidate's photocopy of a diploma or certificate, which could be falsified. Sometimes, of course, there are legitimate reasons why confirming data can't be produced. Institutions of higher learning do close or merge, and records do get lost. Generally however these credentials are about 99 percent verifiable.

Retail Credit Inquiry

Regardless of whether your company is a member of the local retail credit bureau, it is fast and easy to obtain a retail credit check on a person. Bill-paying habits may be important. These reports will tell you about them and also about retail indebtedness, any collection actions, approximate income, financial condition, and sometimes more. In some positions and at some levels in management, this information may be useful to you.

Business Reference Checks

A business reference check is not just a verification of past employment! It is much more. Ask the candidate to provide you with business references who can speak to the subject of past job performance. Ideally this would be the manager the candidate reported to or worked for. In some cases you won't be able to reach him or her but you should try. Let the candidate provide the references but be sure the quality is up to your standards. Try to get a business reference for each job the individual has held in the past ten years. A minimum of four business references is desirable.

Sometimes it may be difficult to locate a reference. Some candidates may not be able to provide references they feel would be favorable from a former employer. As I have indicated before, people leave jobs for all kinds of reasons which have nothing to do with their competency, and some of these partings are not friendly. You will have to be the judge of whether you have the situation covered. When you check a reference by phone, you will want to do the following:

1. Obtain reference's name, company, address, and position held in the company.

2. Determine the basis of reference's acquaintance with the candidate.

3. Ask what position(s) the candidate held.

4. Get observations on job performance. Did the candidate do what he or she claimed in the resume and your interview?

5. Solicit observations on internal upward, peer, and downward relationships.

6. Request observations on any of the success factors discussed in chapter 9. You may want further insights.

7. Describe the position you are seeking to fill. Ask the reference to comment on the candidate's ability to handle it.

8. Ask the reference to comment on the candidate's family life, personal habits, or anything else which might impact on the ability to function effectively in your company. The person will probably hesitate, but ask anyhow.

The purpose of a reference contact is to initiate a full and frank discussion of the candidate's qualifications. I recommend the following opening gambit:

Is this Ed Willes? My name is Marcia Smith, Ed, and I am president of the ABC Company. We are seeking a sales manager and we've had a number of conversations with Tom Brown about the position. We think he is a leading contender, and he has given me your name as a reference. This is a very important job in our organization, Ed, and we owe it to Tom as well as ourselves to be sure we are right for him and he is right for us. I would like to ask you some questions and I would appreciate any insights you would care to provide. Let me be sure I have your name spelled correctly, . . .

A good reference check will take a minimum of twenty minutes. Listen carefully not only to what is said but how it is said. You must draw the references out and get them to talk. Ask questions but don't put words into their mouths. Don't give them your observations and ask them to agree or disagree. Don't ask questions which can be answered "yes" or "no," and don't be afraid to probe for more information. Generally, if you are engaging in your conversation, the references will relax and open up to you. They may, in fact, tell you some things which will surprise you. Get on a first-name basis with the person on the other end of the line from the very beginning. If the names of other people are mentioned in your discussion, note them. You may want to contact them too.

The question will surely arise, "Do I have to do this myself? Can't my personnel department do this?" The answer is yes, you have to do it yourself if the person is going to report to you. No one at this point knows the candidate better than you, and you are the person who has to be satisfied.

In most cases, reference checks will only confirm what you already know. But once in a while, you will get one that will make your palms sweat. That is the one you are looking for. It could save you a bundle.

Criminal Record Checks

Not too long ago, a record of arrest for a felony was the kiss of death for a candidate. It may still be, depending on the circumstances. Assuming, of course that you know about it. In the 1960s and early seventies, many young people exposed themselves to arrest and conviction in Vietnam era protests; some of these were logged on police records as felonies. They need careful evaluation. It is something you will want to discuss candidly with the individual, should your investigation reveal such information.

Police records may also yield information on drunk driving, drug-related incidents, assault and battery, spouse and child abuse, and sex-related offenses, along with a host of other types of aberrant behavior. Don't laugh. It can happen. If you don't want to know about these things, don't do a criminal record check. If you do, however, you will have to get the candidate's permission. Your local police department can tell you what form of release is required by them to disclose these records.

Private Investigative Services

One would have to look a long time to find an occupation more wildly misrepresented in movies and television than that of private investigator. They are portrayed as gun-toting, hard-drinking womanizers when, in fact, they are typically highly trained, skilled, and experienced professionals. Not always, but usually. The good ones are really security consultants, with background and training in federal, state, or local law enforcement plus a thorough knowledge of the law as it applies to investigations and privacy. They are licensed by the state in which they operate (where states require such licensing) and their operations are proscribed by these authorities.

These investigators know the sources of information, how to probe them, and how to interpret the data they yield. They can mount a background check on almost anyone quickly, efficiently, discreetly, and at a relatively modest cost. Usually, they provide a layered approach so the cost will depend on how deeply you want to probe. Investigations can be conducted either overtly or covertly and can cover any or all of the forms of reference mentioned in this chapter, including the checking of business references (although this is one source of information which can be best probed by you).

If you do not want to know the nitty-gritty truth about an individual, do not go to a private investigator. If you do want to go those last few yards to be sure your candidate is not going to be an embarrassment later on, employ an investigator. It may cost you a few hundred dollars, but you will know if there is anything lurking in the candidate's background. Investigators are listed in the yellow pages and are happy to provide credentials and references. Check their references. You will be surprised at who their clients are. The bulk of their work involves exactly what you are talking to them about.

13
Compensation Negotiations
Milestone M

Executive compensation is largely market-driven. If you go into the marketplace to recruit a chief financial officer, for example, you are going to have to pay what CFOs in your type and size of organization are earning these days. There are two dimensions to the executive compensation question. First, what do you have to pay to attract and hold competent, highly motivated people? And second, what can you afford to pay and still control fixed operating costs?

Chapter 2 covered the wisdom of including the compensation range in the position description. Chapter 5 discussed the need to capture salary-progression information. The need to verify the data was described in chapter 12. There is little justification for proceeding to this point in the hiring process without knowing, with a fair degree of certainty, that: (1) you can afford to hire the person you are considering, and (2) that the candidate will accept the position, if offered, in the salary range acceptable to you. That is why it is a good idea to "telegraph" the compensation aspects of the position.

The candidate-development practices described in chapters 4 and 5 should provide an indication of whether the compensation package you are offering is competitive. If it is not, you will have to address the problem early on. Otherwise, you may lose valuable time and also find yourself unable to attract the best qualified people for consideration.

Every executive position has an intrinsic worth to the organization. If you should end up paying more than the midpoint on the salary range, some or all of the following things could happen. All of them are bad.

1. Your fixed operating costs may end up exceeding the budget for the function.

2. You may create dissension within your management ranks by overpaying someone.

3. You may forfeit your ability to reward the individual later on, because he or she is already at the top of the range.

4. You may later feel you were "dry-gulched" in the salary negotiations, to the detriment of your relationship with the individual.

Internal–External Equity

Most companies are keenly aware of the need to maintain internal–external equity (an approximate balance between salaries being paid within the company and what the unique combination of skills, abilities, and experience a position requires is going for in the job marketplace).

There are two ways to deal with this question. One is to roll as much of management compensation as you can into the variable-cost category. That is, find ways to tie executive pay to profitability, return on investment (ROI), or improvements in sales or productivity. Pay for performance. The second way is to make your organization the best place in the industry to work. Give your company ideals, lofty purpose, and corporate pride. Launch a program in which everyone can participate, to strive for operating excellence. If you can build strong company loyalty, you will not have to worry about not being the highest paying company in your industry. Money is not everything.

Always remember that people want something they can believe in and be proud of. Read chapter 3 again.

Candidate Compensation Needs

Critical Path Hiring is designed to provide you with a unique understanding of the person you are considering for an executive position with your company. Consideration of the success factors discussed in chapter 9 tells you, among other things, the degree to which money motivates the candidate, and how important non-monetary motivators are, while providing insight into the life-style and personal goals he or she carries to the bargaining table. Age is also a consideration in the bargaining process. An individual in the thirty- to fifty-year age bracket, with a growing family which must be cared for and educated, may have more need for direct take-home compensation than an older person who would perhaps be in a better position to defer compensation, and would be thinking more in terms of capital accumulation.

Families in which both husband and wife are wage earners (which includes more than 50 percent of the population today) present special compensation-planning problems and opportunities. Your company's knowledge of and willingness to accommodate customized compensation packages can be a big help in the negotiation process. One word of caution is in order. It is a good idea to have any customized compensation package reviewed by your accounting firm to determine the tax consequences to both the employee and the company. Both the U.S. Internal Revenue Service and Tax Court rulings influence the viability of income-deferral and tax-avoidance plans. Your CPA will have the latest interpretations.

Forms of Compensation

In a broad sense, any benefit an employee receives in exchange for services to your company could be considered compensation. In a practical sense, some of these benefits are considered taxable as compensation and others are construed to be nontaxable employee benefits. No effort has been made to distinguish between these in the following examples of compensation.

Monthly or Annual Salary. Direct compensation is usually tied to a salary grade structure for the company and is the base-line pay for services.

Incentives. These can take many forms, depending on company objectives and goals. They can either be awarded on the basis of job performance data or a subjective judgment call by the manager's superior. The usual means is a combination of both. The dollar amount is often expressed as a percent of base salary—30 percent to 40 percent of base for example—in salary negotiations. These incentives include:

Awards based on achievement of MBO goals

Awards based on ratio of budget to actual operating costs

Awards based on actual sales versus planned sales, for sales and marketing functions

Awards for virtually any type of achievement at any level of management

Incentive awards are just that—awards offered as incentives to accomplish specific objectives, usually in a relatively short period of time, quarterly or semiannually. They are designed for short-term achievements. When discussing these awards, it is important to indicate when they are paid.

Bonuses. These are longer-term awards and are usually based on annual performance. They can be designed to discourage actions taken to achieve short-term incentive goals at the expense of the company's long-term interests. Or they can be tied to performance which can only be measured annually. They include:

Bonus pool shares: Sometimes the bonus pool is expressed as a percentage of profits beyond a selected ROI objective. As the net ROI is beyond the control of any one executive, bonuses are usually paid out according to the number of shares each member of the bonus pool group holds. The number of options in such an arrangement are endless.

Annual sales awards: These can be based on raw sales performance, gross margins, net profit, or almost any other basis.

Annual improvement awards: These are based on productivity or any other index of performance which can be measured.

Bonuses are a way of tying everyone's interest to company performance. These are typically cash awards, taxable as ordinary income, and very effective motivators.

Profit-Sharing Plans. These typically involve everyone in the company rather than just the management group. They are usually paid annually according to formulae tied to base-line salary, sometimes extending over several years of employment. Their purpose is twofold: (1) to allow all employees to share in the success of the company, and (2) to make everyone in the company profit-conscious. How successful these plans are at accomplishing this second goal is a moot point. It seems apparent that, unless there is an ongoing program of awareness, they can lose their effectiveness. The reward is just too far in the future to provide a strong incentive for profit-conscious action *today.* Generally, profit-sharing eligibility is not conferred on an employee until after at least one year of employment.

Deferred Compensation Plans. Tax avoidance is an ongoing concern of most executives whose income exceeds their outgo. Do not confuse tax avoidance with tax evasion. Tax avoidance is legal and tax evasion is not. Tax avoidance takes advantage of financial instruments like IRAs and tax shelters to limit taxes on current income by deferring some taxes to a future date when, presumably, the individual will be retired or for other reasons may be in a lower tax bracket. Your CPA firm's tax partner can provide detailed information on the options and alternatives available.

Stock Option Plans. Stock and stock-related forms of compensation are useful tools in motivating management toward the achievement of long-term corporate strategies and goals, ones that may require years to achieve. They may be imperfect tools in this regard, but they are about all you have.

Employee Benefits. These include health and disability insurance, life insurance, vacations and paid holidays, retirement benefits, and tuition-refund plans. They are of vital concern and great value to the candidate. No two company benefit packages are alike.

Executive and Management Perquisites. These include company cars, club memberships of all types, personal or business use of company vehicles and facilities, and personal services paid for totally or in part by the company. To the extent that these perks are used by the individual for business purposes only, they may not be considered as forms of personal compensation. Still, their availability to the candidate is significant.

Relocation Expenses and Front-end Bonuses. If the candidate you are recruiting to your company is currently residing outside the commuting range of the position you are discussing, he or she will have to move home and family. When that happens, someone will incur some or all of the following expenses:

Furniture packing and transfer

Temporary living (until a move can be arranged)

House-hunting trips including spouse

Appraisal of old house

Legal fees on sale of old house

Broker's fee on sale of old house

Bridge loan cost (if required)

Legal expenses for new home purchase

Interim living expenses (while household possessions are in transit)

Mortgage points

Mortgage interest cost differential (if new home carries a higher mortgage rate)

Miscellaneous costs of relocation

If you elect to pay these expenses, some of the payments will be treated by the IRS as ordinary income for the new employee and taxed as such.

It is a good idea to have a company policy where these expenses are concerned and to make candidates aware of what expenses you will and will not cover early on in the discussions. It can easily cost $30,000 to $40,000 to relocate and, if candidates have to shoulder the lion's share of this burden, they may be into the second year of their employment with you before they break even in the compensation game. Failure to reach an understanding on this matter can create a potentially damaging situation with new management employees at the very worst time.

Some companies simply make a front-end lump sum payment, which is intended to cover some but not all of the above costs. It is up to the new employee to spend it as wisely as he can. Such payments can be fairly substantial sums of money, but with the Critical Path Hiring method at least you will have confidence that it is a good investment.

Bonuses and incentives can easily double an executive's direct compensation, while other forms of deferred compensation can offer the opportunity for longer-term capital accumulation. The cost of company benefits packages excluding bonuses are currently running in the 30–40 percent of base salary range. The figure is closer to 40 percent for lower management positions. It is the author's contention that bonuses, incentives, and, in fact, all forms of direct compensation should be awarded as much as possible on the basis of individual performance. This requires that methods of measurement be put in place so that progress can be accurately evaluated.

As pointed out earlier, some individuals are strongly motivated by money and others are not. If you use money to motivate, it is useful to know how effective it can be with a specific person. Some executives seek more money even though they have no compelling need for it and do not support an extravagant life-style. For these people, money is not sought because of its intrinsic value but rather for it psychic reward value. It is their means of keeping score of their value to the organization and their relative worth with their peers, inside and outside the organization.

Employment Agreements

In recent years, corporations have grown more willing to enter into employment contracts with management. While such contracts are more common in some industries than others, and are typically found in high-risk/high-reward positions, their use appears to be spreading. A 1983 study by Ward Howell International reveals that almost half of the largest U.S. corporations now have contracts for top officers.

Critical Path Hiring is designed to give both employer and management employee a high level of confidence that they have made the right choice. Notwithstanding, you may be asked by a leading candidate to offer an employment agreement. Increasingly, such requests are coming not just from candidates for very senior positions but from middle-management as well. How you react to such a request will be governed by how badly you want the individual, by your own personal attitudes, and perhaps also by company policy toward such agreements. Properly structured, such contracts can protect the interests of company and employee alike. The following safeguards from the company's point of view can be established:

1. Compensation, bonus, and benefit arrangements for the period of the contract

2. Separation arrangements, should the manager leave the firm

3. Noncompetition agreement, to prevent raiding by competing firms

4. Confidentiality provisions, also to prevent raiding.

If these matters are important to the company, then a contract may be appropriate.

From the employee's point of view, the following considerations come into play:

1. Job security: No matter how sincerely or thoroughly opportunities are presented, candidates will not truly know if they have been told the whole truth until they have been in the position for a while. They would like the assurance that they will be around long enough to prove their worth and make their move worthwhile.

2. Job continuity: Anyone who leaves one company and position for another knows the hazard of short job tenure.

3. Compensation, bonus, and benefit security

4. Protection from loss of employment due to unforeseen events not related to performance, such as a corporate takeover

5. Clear statement of noncompetition and confidentiality arrangements

These are all legitimate concerns for a new manager. It is the author's contention that Critical Path Hiring will go a long way toward allaying such concerns on the part of the candidate, but perhaps not all the way.

The Ten Commandments of Contracts

Employment contracts are not inherently bad. They may be bad if they are incomplete, unclear, or biased. If you do find yourself in a situation requiring a contract, figure 13–1 provides an excellent guide to what a contract might cover.

One final word. Have your company lawyer draw up the agreement. It is a legally binding contract between the company and the employee.

Job-Offer Letters

Offers of management positions should be put in writing so that candidates have a clear understanding of exactly what they are being offered in the way of compensation. But be careful in writing the letter. Courts have held that a salary expressed in annual terms is a commitment to keep the individual in your employ for at least a year.

Generally, the letter should delineate the compensation factors agreed upon, the terms of employment, and the express statement that employment is at the will of the employer. If specific agreements dealing with nondisclosure of confidential information or noncompetition agreements have been negotiated, these should also be included. At this point, the offer letter comes perilously close to being an employment contract.

It is the author's contention that an employment contract should not be avoided simply because it is a contract. It is better to consciously

> **An employment agreement typically includes eight to ten clauses that cover everything from stock options to dental plans.**
>
> *A Contract*
>
> - 1. **Terms of the agreement.** Three to five years is most common.
> - 2. **The position.** Title and the responsibilities that accompany it.
> - 3. **Base salary.** Subject to periodic review, at least annually.
> - 4. **Annual bonus.** Specifies the form: stock, cash or other.
> - 5. **Long-term incentive awards.** May be stock options, stock appreciation rights, performance share awards, all over several years.
> - 6. **Employee benefits.** Includes: pension, profit-sharing plan, medical and hospitalization plans.
> - 7. **Termination arrangements.** Frequently covers several scenarios:
>   - a) Death. Salary continues for a specified period.
>   - b) Disability. Compensation in excess of employee benefit package.
>   - c) Without cause. Executive disagrees with the board over the company's goals. No misconduct implied. Salary usually continues for one to three years.
>   - d) With cause. Serious misconduct, not just poor performance. All benefits stop.
>   - e) Voluntary termination by the executive. All benefits stop.
>   - f) Golden parachute. A change of ownership or proxy fight results in a change of direction. The executive leaves voluntarily but continues to collect salary or other benefits.
> - 8. **No-compete provisions.** First defines the company's business, then specifies the geographic area and time period in which the executive cannot compete with the business.
> - 9. **Confidentiality provisions.** Governs the preservation of confidential information and prohibits raiding of key employees.
> - 10. **Arbitration.** Court-mandated enforcement of the contract is waived in favor of less costly arbitration. Employer reserves the right to get an injunction in competition or confidentiality disputes.
>
> - *Less formal employment agreements for valued middle managers are usually limited to these clauses.*

Reprinted by permission of *Forbes Magazine*, Feb. 13, 1984. © Forbes, Inc., 1984.

Figure 13–1. *The Ten Commandments of Contracts*

enter into a contractual arrangement with a formal contract than to back into one with a poorly written job-offer letter.

Whichever you elect to do, the important thing is that you provide the candidate with something on which he can base his decision.

The job-offer letter should have a clearly stated expiration time. Usually forty-eight to seventy-two hours is sufficient. It is decision-time for the candidate and time is of the essence. If he or she does not accept, you will want to go on to another acceptable candidate as quickly as possible.

14
Bringing the New Executive into the Company

You've hired a new and highly qualified person to a key position in your company. You're happy; the new recruit is happy. That task is completed. Right? Well, not quite. You still have to bring the individual into the company and get this shining new executive off on the right foot with the rest of the people in the management organization. Aside from the usual routine of filling out forms, passing physical exams, and other necessary busy work, there is a procedure that should be followed whenever a new manager is hired. This chapter is dedicated to a discussion of that procedure. Unlike the Critical Path Hiring procedure, which is highly structured, this part of the employment process is offered in the form of a series of options and alternatives. Your decision to utilize them will depend on the position the new executive will occupy in your organization, your company's structure, your present team, and other considerations.

The notion that a skilled and experienced executive will hit the deck running is naive. The more experienced he or she is, the less likely that person is to hit the deck running. Even if the individual is from the same industry, practically everything is new—a new employer, new policies and procedures, new boss, new organization, new duties, new peers, new staff, new facilities, new products, new problems, and new company politics. If it is a new industry, throw in a couple dozen more "news." If it is in a new city, you can add a new home, new schools, new community, new acquaintances, and new problems and decisions to be made in day-to-day living for the spouse and children.

Hit the deck running? Not on your life. Smart executives will creep around first and find out where the mine fields are laid, which is why you won't realize a whole lot of benefit from them in the first few months of employment. Anything you can do to speed up their learning process will pay big dividends. The following suggestions should help in this regard.

Organizational Information

Before the first day of employment, the new manager should be provided with a package containing the following information.

1. A detailed organization chart of the company should display the company reporting structure, and the name and title of the incumbent in each management position. The new manager's specific area of responsibility should be highlighted.

2. Photographs and a brief profile of each individual at the peer level and above should be provided. If statements of duties and responsibilities of peer executives are available, these should also be included. If you've followed Critical Path Hiring, new executives will know what their own duties are, but they may not know who has responsibility for what outside their own areas. The profiles should cover more than just name, rank, and serial number. They should contain enough to impart a little bit of the other executives' personalities and interests too.

3. As mentioned earlier, financial information has to be shared on a need-to-know basis. Candidates for senior positions will surely want to know the finanicial lion they have to wrestle. You will have to use your own judgment regarding how much financial information can be imparted to new individuals before they are finally behind their desks. Everything about CPH is designed to give you a high level of confidence in the person you hire, but people do sometimes change their minds at the last minute. Yogi Berra's sage advice, "It ain't over 'til it's over," applies. Having a financial information package outside the company may be a risk not worth taking.

In addition, a profile and photograph of the new executive should be distributed to all management people within the company. This can either be done before or at the time the individual begins work. At the very least, peers and those above should receive this profile.

If the advent of the new executive involves a redefinition of the organizational structure, it is better to get these changes and any problems they may create discussed and laid to rest before the new person arrives on the scene. Nothing is more disconcerting than to find yourself in the middle of a jurisdictional dispute your first day on the job.

The Critical First Three Months

How you bring the new executive into your organization will be an important factor in how quickly he or she becomes productive. You have gone to some lengths in the CPH process to present the company as a class act. If you now throw the newcomer to the wolves, you run the risk of unravelling the positive corporate image you've built in his or her mind.

All of the newness for the new executive has to be dealt with as quickly as possible. With appropriate modifications, depending on the level of a new employee in the organization, the following procedures are recommended:

1. The profile of the individual, in press release form with current photograph, should be prepared. It should describe the position briefly and the individual in some depth. This release should be sent to local newpapers and other media and to all applicable trade publications. It may result in free advertising and it represents the company in the best possible way.

2. This press release should be distributed simultaneously to all employees of the company, preferably through a home mailing.

3. Ideally on the first day of employment, a brief meeting of all effected employees should be held, at which time the person who

hired the new executive should introduce him or her and give a short explanation of where the newcomer fits into the organization.

4. Another member of the management team, or another experienced and trusted employee depending on the level of the new hire in the organization, should be assigned to be a big brother or sister to the new employee for the first three months. An appropriate individual for this key responsibility is a senior human resource executive since senior human resource executives generally report directly to the president, and so should be "neutral." It will be his or her responsibility to meet weekly with the newcomer to discuss job progress and any problems the new executive may be encountering. It is also their responsibility to isolate problems before they become crises, and get them resolved.

   When you select the new executive's mentor (angel, protector, confessor, rabbi), be sure to share your observations of the individual's strengths and weaknesses, and your view of the success factors which entered into the hiring decision. He needs to know these things in order to do his job properly.

5. In the first few days of employment, individual meetings with all division or department managers should be set between the new manager and his peers so that he or she can gain a first-hand knowledge of how functions fit together. Too often, these meetings are reduced to a perfunctory introduction in someone's office doorway, and the new executive is left with barely more than a nodding acquaintance with someone he or she will have to work closely with, and with whom he or she shares mutual dependencies.

   It is difficult to imagine how such individual meetings could be completed in an hour or two in a company of any size. They are more likely to require all day, and they should cover the working relationships between the new manager's area of responsibility and the other executive's area, whatever that may be. In addition to learning about how things fit, the manager also needs to get acquainted and begin to build working relationships with the rest of the management team. These meetings will afford the opportunity.

Team building was referred to in the introduction to this book. In chapter 3, it was cited in the context of defining the company. But remember, you cannot talk team and then not act team. This is your opportunity to demonstrate that you really are a team and that the new executive is an important member. If the evaluation you made in the hiring process is accurate, he or she will recognize this and respond positively.

Bonding

What you want to accomplish with the individual in this bringing-on-board phase of employment is bonding. In most employment situations, bonding doesn't take place quickly, and with some people in some situations it never happens. In the context in which it is used here, bonding does not mean fiduciary bonding but rather emotional bonding. It means making a commitment to work together toward accepted and agreed upon goals which are mutually beneficial to both employees and company.

If this can be accomplished, you will have gone a long way toward the objective of creating an environment in which excellence can thrive. In every "world-class" corporate organization that this writer has observed, read about, or been a part of, there has been a strong bond between the corporate entity and the people in it, at all levels in the organization. This does not happen because the president of the company writes a memo saying, in effect, "be a team." It happens because the people are carefully selected to be contributors, and once on board it is made evident that the other employees have a fierce commitment to excellence. That commitment is visible everywhere you look, from the mail boy to the president.

There are three initial steps to establishing a commitment to excellence in a company. They are:

1. Make a commitment yourself. Commit the company, and publish the commitment for all to see, as covered in chapter 3.

2. Make a plan. It needn't be a highly sophisticated document, but it should be detailed enough to provide company goals and objectives.

3. Select people to help achieve the goals and objectives. They should, among other things, have demonstrated a strong willing-

ness to commit their abilities and energies in the past. (Identifying and hiring these kinds of people is what this book is about.)

These are only the initial steps in creating an environment in which
excellence can thrive. Achieving corporate operating excellence involves much more than this. However, these steps must be taken at
the beginning.

The Corporate Challenge

One thing you can almost certainly depend upon is that your new
manager will be challenged early on in the new position. Someone
will want to find out what the new guy is made of. This "blink test"
will come from a peer, and it could come in one of the meetings just
discussed. There is little that you can do to prevent this from happening—and probably little you should do even if you know who
the challenger will be, as you probably do. If you've been correct in
assessing the success factors in the new executive, he or she will defend the challenge like a champion. Strength in the areas of self-
image, goal orientation, and people sense will be most useful in this
defense, but the information you've provided the new executive regarding his or her duties, responsiblities, and authority will also
play a part. What he or she will not know is the personality of the
challenger and how to deal effectively with him or her. The mentor
can be a big help to the new executive in this situation. Mentors
shouldn't intercede in a confrontation, but it can be a big help to
someone new in a company to have a neutral to act as a sounding
board. How effective a mentor can be in such a situation will depend importantly on whether he or she can win the new executive's
confidence and on just how neutral the mentor really is.

Stress Management

The preceding suggestions will help the new executive deal with
some, but not all, of the newness of the situation. It is a time of extreme stress for the new manager, and not coincidentally for the
people who work for him or her. That stress can expand throughout an organization while employees at all levels are learning to deal

with and adapt to the new executive's management style, personality, and learning curve.

At its worst stress can sap productivity and operating effectiveness; it can be damaging to overall employee health; and it can cause turnover at all levels in the company. Yet stress isn't by definition bad. Rather, it is natural and probably unavoidable in management change, since change involves the act of putting aside the old, the known, and the comfortable to venture into the new, the unknown, and the uncomfortable. In such a situation stress can be destructive, but it needn't be. Properly managed, it can be a powerful force for renewal and revitalization. The key is proper stress management.

In recent years, there has been a heightened awareness of stress in business; great progress has been made in methods and techniques for dealing with it. When a new executive is brought into an organization, it is a time for careful observation of a lot of things, one of these being "stress impact." If it becomes apparent and visible in any of the areas mentioned above, it is time to call in a professional stress-therapist to help in coping with the problem.

Easing new executives into your firm can be at least as stressful as finding and hiring them was. But with proper planning, the stress can be controlled and minimized. The next concern is holding onto them.

15
Retaining Top-Flight Executives

It is terribly frustrating and discouraging to assemble a group of exceptionally qualified executives, weld them into a smoothly functioning synergistic management team, and then unexpectedly lose one or more of them to another employer. The efficiency, productivity, and attitude of the whole team can be affected. This book describes a process whereby you can identify and select top-flight executives. But remember, if you can do it, so can others.

Highly successful and highly visible executives average about one telephone call per week from recruiters and would-be employers. The last point to make about Critical Path Hiring is that if you use the process, you should get managers so good they'll be pursued by other companies. There is little you can do to prevent this wooing, but there is a lot you can do to prevent it from being successful.

Now that you have these champs, let's talk for a minute about keeping them. Keeping them is crucial.

The Critical Path Hiring process itself conveys to the newly employed executive the importance the company places on building and maintaining an effective management team. Now the essential follow-through must be made. No company can hope to achieve or maintain a record of excellence in operations unless it attracts and keeps top-flight management. Chapter 4 pointed out that if executives are happy with what they are doing, happy with where they are doing it, happy with what they are being paid, and happy with their forward visibility, they probably will not respond to the blandishments of another potential employer. Skillful recruiters will explore the attitudes of a potential candidate in these areas to look for dissatisfaction. You, as a skillful employer, must assure yourself that they won't find dissatisfaction in your management team.

Job Satisfaction

Several areas of attention bear on the satisfaction an executive receives from his work. They need constant observation.

Duties and Responsibilities. You have provided the manager with a position description which identifies his or her key duties and responsiblities. Presumably, a good deal of thought and consideration went into their definition. Do not usurp them. His or her job satisfaction will come significantly from the successful execution of those duties. It is one reason why the candidate was attracted to the position in the first place. It is also a part of his or her agreement with you. Counsel and advise, but do not usurp.

Review and Evaluation. Defining duties is fine, but the business environment is dynamic, not static. It is a good idea to formally review with the executive at least on a quarterly basis what demands are being made on his or her time, energy, and resources, and how these demands relate to the key areas of responsibility. From time to time, short-term needs may impact on the ability of the manager to cover all the bases. So long as these special demands remain short-term, they can be handled without dislocation, but if they become long-term, think of redefining the position.

Recognition and Reward. Very few people are offended by praise, and even fewer by reward. Chapter 13 deals with the use of short-term monetary incentives, but not every act of recognition needs to be a financial one to be effective. Private praise as well as public recognition among peers and those above can be marvelous boosts to the recipient's self-esteem and job satisfaction. One caveat: spread around the laurels. If praise is showered on one particular person too often, it can be misinterpreted.

Company Satisfaction

If you have adopted a corporate operating philosophy as discussed in chapter 3, you have already taken a giant step toward company satisfaction. This satisfaction relates not just to the management team but to every employee at every level in the organization. It is the author's conviction that people, both individually and as a group, want something to believe in. If they can be persuaded that their employer as a company has lofty purposes, operates ethically, and is sensitive to its employees' interests, they will make a commitment to the firm.

Here are some things that every manager can do to enhance and reinforce that commitment.

Maintain Visibility. Know the team. Be a highly visible presence where the business of the company is taking place. Make employees feel they are working *with* you rather than *for* you. Getting your hands dirty in the work of the company takes a little more effort than you might think. The result, however, is a common bond of understanding, and the knowledge on the part of all the employees that you have an involvement and awareness of what is going on.

Keep the Team Informed. It can be done with a five-minute meeting every morning. Talk about yesterday's achievements in production, quality control, or whatever else is worth mentioning. The employees should feel like they know what's happening. Just remember that the meeting should be positive in spirit, not negative. It isn't necessarily a pep talk, but it has that effect. Above all, it's a talk, not a speech. Positive in substance, brief but supportive.

Celebrate. Find something to celebrate at least once a week. This may sound hokey, but people like to cheer. It is absolutely remarkable how good a rousing cheer can make you feel when it is your team cheering. It may be a significant order, a customer's compliment, a problem solved, a new safety record, an improvement in production, or whatever. Get the whole team together and be a cheerleader. Enthusiasm is infectious.

Create a Competitive Environment. People are by nature competitive creatures. Find a way to bring a spirit of competition into the internal workings of the company. It doesn't matter how corny it is, but there ought to be a trophy (even a big, obscenely gaudy trophy) that gets passed around from group to group within the organization because they have excelled at something. Everyone needs to excel at something.

Recognize Achievement. It is absolutely essential that you recognize the accomplishments of the people on the team. Do it on the spot if possible. In any event the recognition should be as close to the accomplishment as possible. The longer it is delayed, the lesser the impact on the achiever and on everyone else. (The author worked at IBM in the 1950s with a man who sold electric typewriters. He was a top salesman, but he was frustrated because when he sold a typewriter—a hard sell in those days—it was two months before he received a commission. One day he mused that IBM should pay commissions daily. "You should come in at the end of the day and say, 'I sold a typewriter,' and the manager should say, 'Good work, Jim. Here's your $30'." As marvelously well as IBM sold typewriters, it boggles the mind what they would have done with a reward system like that!)

Create a Channel for Ideas. You need channels through which thoughts and ideas about company operations can flow freely from employees to management. It must be done if you are to utilize the last great untapped resource of American industry—the creative ability of the individual employee.

But effectively managing the evaluation of a flow of ideas is a substantial task. Each idea requires some sort of cost-benefit analysis, and even good ideas have to be prioritized to accommodate cash-requirement planning. That is why a manager has to be something of a teacher too. To reject what appears to be on the surface a good idea without explaining why might have the effect of stifling any future contributions. That would be a disaster.

Why are communications between managers and the managed so vital? The reason is simple: managers are one with the people they manage. If employees are happy, managers can be happy; if they are not, managers will not achieve the level of job satisfaction and company satisfaction necessary to sustain a high level of creativity and productivity. Lastly, good managers develop their people. If they do not, they are not good managers—no matter how much you may like them—and they are doing their employer a disservice.

Compensation Satisfaction

Deep satisfaction with the company and the job can offset, to some extent, deficiencies in compensation or benefits. Just how much will depend on the individual and the extent to which he or she is money-driven. If your observations made in assessing the success factors in chapter 9 are correct, you will have a good feel for how susceptible your managers are to juicy outside money offers. Maintaining internal–external equity is difficult, but the effort has to be made. Timely and reliable compensation data is available for almost any position and industry, and the prudent executive will make use of it. Coupled with a fair salary administration system, big gaps between what you are paying and what the job marketplace is dictating can be avoided.

Direct compensation, when wedded with bonuses, incentives, and benefits tailored to the executive's unique needs, can go a long way toward the prevention of management defection to competitors or other industries. But remember, the key to continuity in management is eternal vigilance.

Career Satisfaction

Inevitably you will lose some of your ousthanding performers because of career expectations. There simply isn't that much room at the top. It is the price you have to pay for high achievers. The greatest challenge of upper management is to keep the next lower level of management challenged and thereby motivated. There are two possible solutions to the problem of career paths for upper-level executives. One of them is to follow the selection procedures advocated in Critical Path Hiring and then encourage them toward greater professionalism and growth at every opportunity. The other is to surround yourself with average performers—and the consequences of that are too awful to contemplate.

Appendix A
Sample Position Descriptions

SAMPLE POSITION DESCRIPTION

Company: GOF, Incorporated
                       9999 Maria Street
                       City One, State One

Position: Vice President of Manufacturing

Position Overview:

The vice president of manufacturing is accountable to the chief executive officer for all manufacturing and assembly operations of the company. As indicated elsewhere in the information you have received, GOF is a manufacturer of precision HVAC equipment for application in general industry and nuclear power generating facilities. It is a contractor to the Department of Defense in the construction of U.S. Navy surface vessels and submarines. Our manufacturing operations are carried on in three facilities located in Montclair, N.J., Round Lake, Ill. and Seattle, Wash.,and employ approximately 550 hourly workers. Two of the facilities are organized under the United Autoworkers, with which we have an acceptable relationship. Over the past five years we have made diligent efforts to automate our fabrication and assembly operations wherever possible, but much remains to be done. Manufacturing consists of sheet metal operations, plastics molding, FRP operations, and assembly of electrical and electronic components. Outside sourcing of this last area is followed wherever possible. Our primary focus in these areas is to continue to reduce fixed costs in P&E, inventory, and labor.

Duties and Responsibilities:

1.   Acting upon sales department data, and with the assistance of plant and production managers, establish and maintain an orderly and cost-effective production schedule and flow which maximize the utilization of plant, equipment, and labor resources, while respecting customer order commitments. Production is approximately 50 percent to order and 50 percent to inventory.

2.   With the manager of plant engineering, launch an immediate review of all material-handling and fabricating operations to determine what immediate improvements can be made with existing facilities and to determine cost versus benefits of automation. Prepare a progress report and recommendations for executive committee consideration within 120 days of employment, and quarterly reviews thereafter.

3.   With purchasing department, establish a review system to rate vendor performance, review all existing commitments to purchase, and evaluate inventory levels for all raw materials and components. Purchasing is now decentralized. Explore the feasibility of centralization and prepare quarterly reports of inventory-investment efficiency for the executive committee. Raw-material inventory investment at present production levels must be reduced 12 percent in the new fiscal year.

4. With sales management, review and adjust finished-goods inventory levels and production lead times to reflect current order rates and marketplace conditions. Maintain a close and continuous liaison to assure the responsiveness of the company within targeted gross profit margins. Assure that communications between sales and manufacturing are working.

5. With human resources department, assure that all labor agreements are observed. Worker morale is an ongoing concern. Develop programs to cross-train employees wherever possible, and launch an immediate evaluation of the quality circle and suggestions programs. They are not working. Absenteeism is slowly rising. Reverse this trend.

6. With the chief financial officer, launch a thorough review of the current operating budget to identify any possible areas of further containment and reduction in manufacturing costs. Review the present standards and cost-accounting system and establish new standards where necessary for value added in production.

7. Our expensive production-management (bill of materials processor) and control system is a disappointment. Find out why and present our options and alternatives to the executive committee by the end of this fiscal year.

8. Explore the feasibility of combining plant engineering, sales engineering, and the product development lab under a director of engineering to report to you. Prepare a report with the sales and financial departments to the executive committee incorporating your joint recommendations.

9. Evaluate current quality control methods, procedures, and standards. Our fabricated parts and subassemblies must mate in the field. When they do not, it is a costly embarrassment. It happens too often. There have also been sporadic breakdowns in the quality of purchased materials. These areas need continuous attention.

10. The vice president of manufacturing sits on the executive committee, the product planning committee, and the community relations committee. In addition, he or she may be called upon to conduct acquisition evaluations, and other special duties at the discretion of the board of directors, the president, and the chief executive officer.

Skills and Abilities Required

A demonstrated ability to organize and manage a multiplant metal fabrication operation efficiently and effectively.

The skill and knowledge to control manufacturing operations involving both production and job shop work on an integrated, cost-effective basis.

The ability to deal effectively and harmoniously with other departments to further the total interests of the company.

Proven ability to anticipate, budget, and control direct and indirect manufacturing costs, inventory investments, and capital expenditures.

The ability to communicate effectively at all levels of the manufacturing organization, and provide strong, decisive leadership.

Education, Knowledge, and Experience Required

An undergraduate degree in manufacturing management is desirable but not essential. Some college or technical school training is acceptable if accompanied by specialized education in the areas listed below, and if supported by successful hands-on work experience in relevant manufacturing management.

Knowledge and experience in the following areas: plastics molding and fabrication, statistical quality control, production planning and scheduling (utilizing computer MRP/BOMP system), standard cost accounting and group incentive systems, and materials management and purchasing.

A minimum of ten years of manufacturing supervision and management is essential. At least five years must have been in a union environment.

Reporting Structure:

The vice president of manufacturing is accountable to the chief executive officer for administration of the manufacturing operations and facilities of the company.

The following managers report directly to the vice president of manufacturing, who is responsible for their operations:

Plant Managers at Montclair, Round Lake, and Seattle

Manager-Plant Engineering

Manager of Product Development

Manager of Quality Control

Materials Manager

The vice president of manufacturing has a peer relationship with: vice president of sales, vice president-chief financial officer, and vice president-administration and field operations.

Profit Responsibility:

Specific performance and profit goals, associated with manufacturing and overall company objectives, will be communicated in detail as discussions progress.

Special Requirements:

Substantial travel between the three plant locations may be expected. The vice president must maintain a highly visible presence and close involvement in company manufacturing activities. Some involvement in the negotiations of large contracts, primarily government, may be expected. Representation of the company in various trade associations and standards committees is required. Some presence in the civic and social life of City One is required.

<u>Compensation</u>:

Base compensation is in the $90,000/year range and is reviewed annually.

Bonuses and incentives, based on agreed-upon objectives under the control of manufacturing management, up to a maximum of 35 percent of base, are awarded for successful performance. Bonuses are paid in the year following award. Other short-term incentives may be offered at the discretion of the president.

A comprehensive employee benefits program includes: twice annual base life insurance, three weeks of annual vacation, fully paid health, major medical, dental, and vision insurance; and college tuition refund.

A noncontributory employee retirement plan is offered. In addition, a 401-k plan is available.

A company car and use of a company-owned vacation lodge near Seattle are available.

<u>Location</u>:   Company Headquarters
                       City One, State One

SAMPLE POSITION DESCRIPTION

<u>Company</u>:   ABC Fastener Company
            Any Street
            Any City, Any State

<u>Position</u>:   Regional Sales Manager

ABC manufactures and markets a broad line of fastener products for use in the fabrication and assembly of metal and plastic products. The company sells its products through dealers and distributors and, in some specialized instances (engineered products), on a direct basis.

<u>Duties and Responsibilities</u>:

1.   Establish and maintain a close working relationship with all company dealers and distributors in the assigned region. This includes owners as well as product line managers of these organizations.

2.   Establish a sales relationship through the dealer/distributor organization with any customer whose purchases of our products exceed an amount specified by the national sales manager; also with any customer of engineered products.

3.   In cooperation with the national sales manager, set annual sales and profit goals for your region and allocate sales and profit quotas by product line and subproduct line to the dealers and distributors in your area. Also set minimum inventory levels by distributor by subproduct line.

4.   Monitor all orders from dealers in your region on a monthly basis to assure an acceptable level of sales activity. Monitor all stock-replenishment orders by distributors to assure minimum acceptable stock levels.

5.   Immediately follow up on any extraordinary sales activity. Investigate and report findings to the national sales manager.

6.   Respond immediately to any product-quality problems or application difficulties reported in your region. Investigate and provide a written report including estimated financial impact and recommended course of action to the national sales manager and to the product engineering department. Monitor and participate in all action programs. You are responsible for customer satisfaction!

7.   Visit each distributor at least quarterly and each dealer at least twice per year. You are the primary interface with the sales organization. All correspondence, credit, and collection will flow through you.

8.   On a quarterly basis, conduct a one-week sales training seminar for all new salespersons in your dealer/distributor organization. This program is to be planned and executed by you, with assistance from product engineering where required.

9.   Make calls with salespeople and continuously monitor dealer/distributor effectiveness. Report in writing each quarter. With approval of national sales manager, terminate and employ new dealers and distributors.

10.   Continuously monitor all competitive products and marketing activities. Report in writing monthly to the national sales manager and product engineering department.

11.   Follow up immediately on any inquiry regarding engineered products and, with the assistance of product engineering, prepare and present required proposals.   The sales responsibility is yours, not engineering's.

12.   Refer any product-pricing questions which fall outside published prices and your discretionary limits to the national sales manager for resolution.

Reporting Structure:

Position reports to national sales manager. Position manages dealer/distributor sales network.

Skills and Experience Requirements:

Sales: A minimum of five years of successful field sales experience in industrial products.

Distribution: Knowledge and experience in selling through motivating and managing a dealer, distributor, or manufacturer's representative sales network. Experience in working in one of these organizations in an outside sales capacity will be considered.

Technical: Although not an absolute requirement, some knowledge of the fastener business as it applies to the manufacture of metal and plastic products would be a definite plus.

Territory: Some knowledge and contacts in the metal and plastic fabrication industry in the region indicated would be pluses but are not absolute requirements.

Other: Well-developed sales skills, both oral and written communications skills, and the ability to make effective sales presentations are absolutely essential. Experience in formal sales training would be a plus.

Education and Training Requirements:

Some college-level education is required for this position. An undergraduate degree would be a plus if it is in business administration, management, or manufacturing engineering.

A combination of formal sales training, technical school training, and direct relevant sales experience in fasteners may be acceptable in place of college experience.

Compensation:

Direct compensation is a combination of salary, commissions, and bonuses based on sales and profit objectives. Salary is in the $2,100 to $2,500/month range, based on qualifications. Commissions and bonuses average in the $800 to $1,200/month range and are a percentage of net sales. There is no ceiling on commissions, which are paid quarterly.

The company provides hospitalization and major medical insurance, two weeks of paid vacation upon completion of one full year of employment, and paid holidays, as designated by the company.

A company car and company-paid expense account for business use are provided.

Life insurance is company-paid in the amount of two times annual salary.

Travel and Location:

The company expects that the regional manager will take up residence near the geographic center of the region. It will pay relocation costs for such a move in accordance with the established policy for new employees. The company will also pay for any telephone and clerical services costs incurred in maintaining an office in home.

It is expected that 60 to 70 percent travel will be required by the position.

Regional Responsibility:

New England and New York state east of Interstate Route 81 (including Binghamton and Syracuse).

SAMPLE POSITION DESCRIPTION

Company: Green Scene Lawn Care, Incorporated
1111 Blue Grass Lane
City One, State One

Position: President and Chief Executive Officer

Position Overview:

The president is accountable to the board of directors for the day-to-day operation of the company. The company has grown rapidly over the past five years. In some areas, the internal operating systems and controls have not kept pace with this growth. In addition, the employees (70 percent of whom have been with the company less than two years) appear to lack long-term commitment. Although the company has operated profitably in the past three years, the return on invested capital has not been acceptable; increased competition coupled with the declining economy leads the board of directors to believe that steps must be taken now to improve the cost effectiveness of operations. At present, the business of the company is seasonal. Activities must be found to effectively utilize the company's resources, especially the people resource, during off-season. In addition to strengthening our position in our primary markets (residential and commercial lawn care), the board believes a purposeful program to explore methods of broadening the company's revenue base should be considered.

Duties and Responsibilities:

1. With the assistance of the chief financial officer, define, develop, review, and control such internal operating systems as are required to achieve budgetary and financial-planning objectives. This includes not only the ongoing evaluation of agreed upon targets for overall company operations in the areas of sales and net income, equity per share, and income per share, but also the continuous review, protection, and enhancement of corporate assets and their utilization to achieve productivity goals and overall improvement.

2. With sales and marketing management, define, develop and implement plans and programs which, coupled with high quality products and service, will assure the satisfaction of customers and the preservation, continuity, and expansion of the company's revenue base.

3. With human resources management, establish and maintain such policies and practices as are required to improve employee attitude, morale, and identification with the operating objectives of the company. Particular attention should be paid to the retention of middle and senior management people who have the ability to develop their own competitive services. A formal program proposal treating on the areas of improved communications, incentives, and the opportunity for management to exercise entrepreneurial interests within the company should be prepared for board consideration as quickly as possible.

4. Assure that product and services research and development resources and funds are adequate and that activities are focused on and in step with the growth and marketplace requirements of the company.

5. With field operations and R&D management, regularly evaluate level of service, adequacy of delivery systems, and cost-effectiveness of product delivery to customers. Institute periodic formal board presentations on alternative product and delivery systems utilizing state-of-the-art product and technology developments.

6. Evaluate the effectiveness, useful life, and consequences of terminating such company business-development programs as Project Overseed, Operation Outreach, and Dandy-Crab. Develop effective means to measure cost versus benefits of such future programs.

7. Review, appraise, and prepare for board consideration a report on the structure and effectiveness of the company organization. Particular attention should be paid to the areas of management control, responsiveness, internal communications, and effectiveness of individual management personnel. It is expected that if required, a revised organization plan with specific recommendations be presented within the fiscal year just beginning.

8. Develop for board approval a <u>Statement of Corporate Operating Philosophy</u>. This document should address such areas of concern as customer interests, stockholder interests, employee interest and obligations, and community responsibility. This document will be for wide public dissemination and should provide the ethical framework and basis for the business conduct and future dealings of the company and its people.

9. Establish a timely and effective means of monitoring competitive activity as it relates to advertising and sales, product-effectiveness, delivery-system-effectiveness, and pricing. Assure that company management is continuously aware and that effective countermeasures are applied.

10. The company currently purchases all fertilizers, herbicides, and insecticides formulated to our unique specifications from outside vendors for the geographic areas in which we operate. Our exposure to faulty formulation and lapses in quality control is great. Assure that such breakdowns in control do not occur. Continuously monitor the effectiveness of internal QC measures to minimize company exposure.

11. The company currently operates under a limited number of franchise arrangements in selected geographic areas. The cost-effectiveness, profit potential, and control aspects of these arrangements are as yet undetermined. Evaluate the viability of franchising as a means of achieving future growth and present for board consideration your recommendations within the fiscal year.

12. Administer the day-to-day operations of the company and its people providing a visible, motivated, involved, and enthusiastic leadership model. Strive to translate the previously mentioned <u>Statement of Corporate Operating Philosophy</u> into action programs which embrace not only the company but also the communities in which we operate.

<u>Skills and Abilities:</u>

Proven administrative skills gained in a service-oriented, consumer-oriented environment are absolutely essential. The management system in place in the company is participative.

Well-developed communication skills, both oral and written, are required. The president of Green Scene is the chief company spokesperson. He or she will be expected to maintain a high-visibility presence both inside and outside the company.

Proven financial-planning, management, and budget-control knowledge and experience are required.

A well developed sense of organizational dynamics coupled with motivational skills, people-sensitivity, and strong leadership ability are essential.

A demonstrated ability to develop and implement imaginative and creative plans, programs, and new approaches to old problems and new opportunities, coupled with the ability to anticipate and act, rather than to recoil and react, is necessary.

Training, Education, and Experience:

An undergraduate degree in science is a minimum requirement. The undergraduate degree may be in engineering, education, or liberal arts if it is coupled with a graduate degree in business administration or administrative sciences, or significant formal additional training in management.

Formal management development training with a previous employer would be a plus.

Successful progression through a variety of lower, middle, and upper management positions, totalling a minimum of ten years, is required. This experience must include a position with limited or preferably, full Profit and Loss responsibility for a minimum of three years.

Knowledge and experience in the management of a service-oriented, consumer-oriented company operating on a multi-office, multi-city basis is required.

Reporting Structure:

The president is accountable to the board of directors for the successful operation of the company.

The following corporate officers report directly to the president, who is responsible for them:

Treasurer/Chief Financial Officer
Vice President/Human Relations
Vice President/Sales and Marketing
Vice President/Operations
Vice President/Research and Development

Profit Responsibility:

Specific performance and profit goals of the company, based on the company financial plan, will be communicated in detail as discussions progress.

Special Requirements:

As indicated elsewhere, the company is organized on a regional basis, with substantial accounting and operational functions carried on in the four regional offices. Experience indicates that the president should spend a substantial amount of time, both business and personal, in these locations to effectively deal with the company's business.

In addition, an active presence in the civic and social life of City One is required.

Compensation:

Base compensation is in the $175,000/year range and is reviewed annually.

Bonuses and incentives, based on objectives and aggregating 65 percent of base salary, are awarded for successful performance.   Other awards may also be made at the discretion of the board.   Bonuses are paid in the year following award.

Deferred compensation may be arranged.   (No retirement plan currently exists.)

Stock options are available.

A liberal life insurance program is available.

A liberal employee benefits package including four weeks of paid vacation; fully paid health, major medical, dental, and vision insurance; and college tuition refund is offered.

A company car plus country and athletic club memberships are provided.

Location:

Company Headquarters
City One, State One

Appendix B
Corporate Operating
Philosophy Examples

THE NATIONWIDE® PHILOSOPHY

where it started   /   how it grew   /   what it means for the future

NATIONWIDE'S PRINCIPLES AND OBJECTIVES

We believe that people have within their own hands the tools to fashion their own destinies.

We believe that by working together people can develop an economy of abundance which will provide a maximum of opportunity, freedom, and security for all.

Motivated by these principles, and with an abiding faith in the worth and dignity of every human being, the Boards of Directors of the Nationwide Insurance Companies have adopted the following objectives as the official guide for the administration and operation of the Companies:

1 To provide people — individually and in groups — with the highest quality insurance and financial services for their economic and personal welfare; and to provide these services at the lowest possible cost consistent with the maintenance of efficiently operated, financially sound, growing companies.

2 To invest policyholder and shareholder funds so as to build financial security, and at the same time make a meaningful contribution to fulfillment of human and social needs.

3 To operate as consumer-oriented companies whose products and services reflect high sensitivity to the changing wants and needs of people.

4 To further business practices which are fair and equitable to policyholders, shareholders, agents, employees, and the public.

5 To encourage customers to participate in the activities of the companies.

6 To invite the active sponsorship of groups of people joined together for their mutual achievement and benefit.

7 To provide Nationwide employees and agents with opportunities and incentives for self-expression and personal growth — in economic stature, in mind, and in spirit.

8 To act as a good corporate citizen by participating responsibly in economic, social, and industry matters affecting the public interest.

Original Home Office Building

The Nationwide® Organization

Nationwide Mutual Insurance Company
Nationwide Mutual Fire Insurance Company
Nationwide Life Insurance Company
Nationwide General Insurance Company
Nationwide Property and Casualty Insurance Company
Colonial Insurance Company of California
Farmland Insurance Company
Nationwide Communications, Inc.
Nationwide Development Company
Nationwide Financial Services, Inc.
Nationwide Corporation

OUR BACKGROUND

THE NATIONWIDE FAMILY of companies originated with the idea that people can satisfy their economic wants and needs — and do it less expensively and usually more satisfactorily — by pooling their resources and working together through organizations they themselves own and control.

In 1919 Ohio farmers established the Ohio Farm Bureau Federation and set about marketing their products and purchasing their fertilizer, feed, and other farm supplies cooperatively. In 1926, following the same pattern, they formed the Farm Bureau Mutual Automobile Insurance Company. Thus, they were able to provide for themselves a needed service at prices they could afford.

The insurance plan worked out so well that the service was expanded to urban people and to other states.

To meet other insurance and security needs, these farmer-consumers formed their own fire insurance company and took over a life insurance company. Later, these user-owned companies provided, through subsidiary and affiliated companies, such services as credit, mutual funds, housing, mortgage financing, urban redevelopment, and radio and television communication. Eventually, in 1955, the companies' name was changed to Nationwide Insurance to facilitate expansion coast to coast.

People's needs come first

For the most part, the organizations making up the Nationwide institution were established to fill a general need existing, or thought to exist, at the time they were formed. This was the down-to-earth Farm Bureau kind of thinking which produced so many successful farm cooperatives, and which today explains Nationwide's continuing interest in cooperative organizations and development. It also explains Nationwide's early rapid expansion in various states through sponsoring organizations. Nationwide's sponsors were, and have been, cooperative associations or cooperative-type organizations that wanted to make insurance available to their members at the most reasonable cost possible. They recommended Nationwide Insurance to their members, and the insurance companies grew rapidly.

Nationwide, of course, is not a cooperative and never has been. All insurance companies in the United States are organized legally under a different set of laws from those governing cooperatives. But it is important to recognize that the underlying cooperative philosophy — the idea of people joining together to provide themselves with goods and services at cost — has been, and continues to be, deeply embedded in the thinking of Nationwide's policymaking people, and of many of the companies' other employees and agents.

The specific principles and practices of this philosophy, as set down for cooperatives, are: open membership; democratic control; distribution of savings in proportion to patronage; lim-

ited interest on share capital; political and religious neutrality; cash trading; and promotion of education among members, employees, and the general public.

Although no exact measurement is possible, we know that this philosophy has contributed greatly to our record of accomplishment. Assuredly, the Nationwide companies have done quite well during their first half century in business according to most standards of success. It is certainly a major accomplishment to serve the financial security needs of over 4.5 million policyholders and to amass more than $4 billion in assets.

Changes ahead

Today, with business at a crossroads, we recognize that Nationwide's choice of future direction depends on our reaction to today's social and economic conditions. Obviously we are living in a world that's on fire. People on all continents have come to realize that the conditions under which most of them have been living can be changed. Through revolution, through military actions, through riots, boycotts and other concerted actions, people are striving to improve their lot. The struggle between differing political ideologies — the developing differences between supposedly like systems — will be with us far into the future. And this turbulence will be accompanied by economic, social, and cultural changes.

Here in America we have seen major changes during the past century, and now we're in the midst of a social revolution, the end of which is years and years ahead of us. One of the manifestations of this social revolution is the intensified interest people are displaying in organizing to protect their interests as consumers. There is much reason to believe their influence as consumers will greatly increase in the future.

OUR COOPERATIVE ORIENTATION TODAY

OUR COMPANY PHILOSOPHY was never actually stated in writing until after World War II. About 1948 the first statement of principles and objectives was adopted. Revisions were studied and adopted in the early 1960s. The Board of Direc-

tors approved a revised statement of Principles and Objectives in January, 1965, and again in 1972. These subsequently were communicated to all employees and agents.

One of these objectives is: "To invite the active

sponsorship of groups of people joined together for their mutual achievement and benefit." This objective, along with our close association with cooperatives, has prompted questions about our being a "cooperatively-oriented" institution. What do we mean by it? How does it fit in with the way we do business today?

The following statements demonstrate what we mean today when we say Nationwide is "cooperatively oriented."

Though the word "cooperative" is not used in Nationwide's principles and objectives, they closely resemble and emphasize the same ethical, moral, and human values that cooperatives seek to emphasize. That people can "fashion their own destinies" by "working together" ranks high as a cooperative concept. This is restated in Nationwide objective "To operate as consumer-oriented companies. . ." Likewise, our objective "To encourage customers to participate . . ." is similar to the cooperative aim for membership participation. And the objective "To invite the active sponsorship of groups of people joined together for their mutual achievement and benefit" puts out the welcome mat for cooperatives.

Summed up, our principles and objectives say that Nationwide exists to help people help themselves. This is precisely the purpose of a cooperative. A co-op is a business owned by the people who use it and operated in their behalf. So is Nationwide. Moreover, Nationwide maintains both business and philosophical ties with cooperatives and our association with them is potentially a strong, expanding, developing, and motivating force.

This force can strengthen and help us put into practice our corporate aim "to operate as consumer-oriented companies." It can establish Nationwide as an organization that's on the side of the people, an organization concerned with helping people to help themselves. And it can help establish Nationwide as "a friend of the family" and therefore as a leader in providing financial security opportunities for the American people.

Sponsors and endorsers

Nationwide's sponsors and endorsers, moreover, are groups having a distinct consumer orientation. Some of these groups are definitely

organized as cooperatives; others as cooperative in many of their principles and practices. Even such endorsers as state government employee associations often are motivated by their members' mutual interests as consumers.

Historically, our sponsor organizations have performed three separate and distinct functions:

1. They have been a means of advancing the processes of cooperative education and organization. Thus, sponsorship has been a cooperative development program.

2. They have provided a quick and efficient method of extending insurance services to large new markets. Thus, sponsorship has been a marketing program.

3. They have provided cooperative leaders to serve on our Boards of Directors. Thus, sponsorship became our governing program.

Upon a re-examination of these sponsorship functions in the light of changing economic, social, and insurance trends, and trends in Nationwide itself, in November 1966, our Board of Directors developed and approved the following recommendations:

1. That where organizations at present are effectively *sponsoring* Nationwide Insurance, such sponsoring arrangements should be continued.

2. That in the future, only those organizations should be engaged as sponsors which contribute specifically and significantly to sponsorship functions — cooperative development, insurance marketing, recommending of qualified Board candidates, and such other requirements as the Board may from time to time determine.

3. That Nationwide develop *endorsing* arrangements with selected cooperative, occupational, and professional associations which are multiplying and expanding in the United States today.

4. That the Board Sponsors Committee and the Office of Public Relations start an immediate search for potential sponsor groups that can serve Nationwide; bringing new policyholders to Nationwide; and that there be a continuing search for new endorser groups for Nationwide products.

5. That in the future the search for sponsors not be limited to cooperatives or agricultural groups, but shall include large urban groups and interested groups of consumers.

The Nationwide Board reaffirmed sponsor/endorser activities in 1976.

It is obvious from the directors' recommendations, and from a realistic examination of the economic factors involved, that we must continue to broaden our concept of consumer groups. And at the same time we have to recognize the potential for serving people's needs by working through dynamic, creative, growing cooperative organizations.

EMPHASIS FOR THE FUTURE

NATIONWIDE's first objective is:

"To provide people — individually and in groups — with the highest quality insurance and financial services for their economic and personal welfare; and to provide these services at the lowest possible cost consistent with the maintenance of efficiently operated, financially sound, growing companies."

This objective recognizes that, over the years, our service has not been limited to members of cooperatives, nor, for that matter, to any kind of membership group. Our concern for people as individuals, which imparts a certain openness to Nationwide's thinking and development, has led us to a variety of approaches to serving people. We have reached them through their cooperatives, through our agency force, through other groups, through employees, and even through government.

Customers and consumers

Today, when business in general is showing increased interest in customers as consumers, we are proud that Nationwide's philosophy has always considered the consumer's needs as business's reason for being. It remains only for us to place increased emphasis on the consumer orientation covered in our third corporate objective — "To operate as consumer-oriented companies whose products and services reflect high sensitivity to the changing wants and needs of people."

Consumer orientation means that every product we sell, every service we offer, every move we make is first examined from the consumer's viewpoint in relation to his actual wants and needs. It means that satisfaction from the consumer's point of view must always be a prime consideration over those products and services which serve the company, management, or employee point of view.

There is evidence that the company which follows the above course of consumer orientation will become the leader of our industry. In fact, the very survival of our industry may hang on this business approach.

This approach fits in perfectly with the emphasis we have been placing on excellence in customer service. We have been stressing that there is no more important group of people in the world than that group of consumers whose needs we are already filling — our customers. We have also been aware that we must continue to search for all conceivable ways to satisfy their needs so well that they will want to remain our customers.

Our philosophy aligns us not only with the customer, but with tens of millions of consumers who are not yet our customers. Hence, we recognize that we must be consumer oriented.

This emphasis on consumer orientation is compatible with our sixth corporate objective — "To invite the active sponsorship of groups of people joined together for their mutual achievement and benefit."

Historically, our very origin and rapid growth points out the great advantage of working with groups, in our case mostly cooperative or cooperatively-oriented groups. We need only broaden our interpretation of what constitutes a group of people.

In the future it should mean not only a cooperative group, but any group of people joined together to avail themselves of some product or service that will improve their conditions of life — with the one further stipulation that the group is generally compatible with Nationwide's principles and objectives. This would include such diversified groups as a state employees association, a bar association, a medical association, a credit union, or any other of those rapidly forming associations whose consumer members have needs that can be filled by Nationwide products or services.

Employees, agents, and citizens

No examination of Nationwide's philosophy would be complete without considering it in the context of our seventh and eighth corporate objectives, namely — "To provide Nationwide employees and agents with opportunities and incentives for self-expression and personal growth — in economic stature, in mind, and in spirit" and "To act as a good corporate citizen by participating responsibly in economic social, and industry matters affecting the public interest."

These two objectives express our companies' most fundamental philosophy — the concern for people *as people*. We have a personal concern for the welfare of our agents and employees. What serves the company as a corporate entity must serve them as individuals, must give them increased opportunity for satisfying work and success. Thus, when we make special efforts to communicate to the Nationwide family and to the public what we stand for and what we are trying to accomplish, we are, in effect, providing growth opportunities for our agents and employees. For the result of this communication of our philosophy can only increase the avenues of service in which our agents and employees can participate and reap benefit.

Concern for people is also evident in Nationwide's expressed desire to act as a good corporate citizen. In many ways and especially in recent years, the company has done an excellent job in its role as a corporate citizen. The companies, and our agents and employees as a group, have demonstrated responsible citizenship — even leadership — in many programs for the social, economic, and cultural improvement of people. Examples include: the company's participation in

United Fund campaigns; the company's civic leadership in our home office community and in varying degrees in our regional communities; the agent-employees' Central American CARE program; our leadership and participation in industry affairs.

So our philosophy of helping people help themselves fits in perfectly with good corporate citizenship, and deserves emphasis. In acting on our philosophy, our work as a corporate citizen must be continued, even improved upon, in the realization that we have a responsibility to people to improve their world, and bring about an improved climate in which to serve them. The needs of people locally, nationally, and internationally will be better served as the world in which they live finds a way to improve the well-being of people everywhere.

Measure for success

In summary, an evaluation of our institutional philosophy shows it has had a definite impact on our business success and will continue to provide a strong directive for our future.

Looking backward, we see that we started as an institution involving a group of people who had needs to be served and we geared our products and services to those needs. Consequently, we should know better than many businesses that starting with a consumer's need and helping him find the most economical way to fill that need is a highly successful way to do business. The basic institutional beliefs and goals that have motivated Nationwide seem to be the ideal way for people to improve their lot.

Looking forward, we recognize that our broad direction for the future should encompass a re-emphasis of our consumer and cooperative orientation, in which we measure every product and every service that we offer on the basis of how well it will serve consumer needs.

NATIONWIDE INSURANCE / AFFILIATED COMPANIES / NATIONWIDE CORPORATION

> **❝** *A meaningful corporate value structure should encourage a behavioral/ decision making environment which causes us to achieve our purpose.* **❞**

Introduction

This statement is intended to provide our shareholders, employees, prospective employees, licensees and all those who do business with us, with an understanding of the kind of organization Ponderosa, Inc. is. It represents the principles and philosophies upon which we shall conduct our affairs. While we will be judged primarily by our actions, this statement should add direction and meaning to our work.

Ponderosa, Inc. is a diversified company that competes in various segments of the foodservice industry, the largest private employer in the United States. Foodservice is highly competitive and provides a striking example of the dynamic society in which we live.

Ponderosa is proud to be a part of this industry. It is a challenge to face skilled competitors and to succeed or fail on the basis of our management competence.

As a company, we will strive to be the best managed in every possible way. Accomplishment of that goal calls for vision, flexibility, honesty and the capability to develop our human resources. We not only must be good planners, but we must be good doers.

We still are a young company, with many things to improve upon. We have learned that we must be innovative and open-minded in all areas. We must constantly explore, develop and plan in all areas if we are to keep our organization sound and growing.

The critical ingredients involved in achieving these results and in building our Company are the individuals employed, the way in which they communicate with each other and the way they manage. Our people will shape the future of Ponderosa, Inc., and the quality of that future will be determined by how well we work together while maintaining our own individuality and creativity.

continued

We encourage our employees to carefully read this statement in order to assess the degree to which their personal goals and Ponderosa's are compatible. Only when they are, can the greatest personal satisfaction and accomplishment be achieved.

I believe it is necessary that we publish our philosophy and emphasize the importance which our Board of Directors, the senior management, and I, personally, attach to it. I sincerely welcome your thoughts about it.

Sincerely,

Gerald S. Office, Jr.
Chairman of the Board
and President

Ponderosa's Purpose

The basic purpose of Ponderosa, Inc. is to achieve results which protect and increase the long-term value of our shareholders' investment. By serving this commitment, we will be able to satisfy the needs of our other constituents including licensees, employees and the communities in which we do business.

The enhancement of our shareholders' investment requires that we achieve and maintain a high rate of return on our employed capital and shareholders' equity, which will help generate the financial resources we need to grow; consistent earnings growth, at rates above inflation; and a strong financial position.

We will achieve these objectives by providing high quality and service to our customers in each of the business segments in which we compete; by maintaining an organization which places a balanced emphasis on careful planning and consistent execution; by managing our physical assets in a prudent, yet progressive manner; and by allocating our resources strategically to attain the growth in profits we seek. Just as importantly, we will strive to maintain high standards of excellence among our employees by encouraging personal development and by recognizing the value of each individual to our organization.

Our corporate objectives and strategies are incorporated by reference into this document. It must be recognized that only by a successful blending of our financial goals and the values stated herein, can we achieve our purpose.

What We Stand For

Ponderosa, Inc. recognizes that the competitive environment in each of the various business segments in which we compete is unique and must be managed accordingly. However, there is one important standard which applies to all our businesses and is critical to our success.

That standard is excellence, to be the best at what we do. Our challenge is to meet this standard by providing high-quality services and products on a consistent basis.

The Company's success will depend on professional management skills supported by an entrepreneurial spirit. We strive to maintain a climate which will encourage competent, productive, innovative and profit-motivated persons to produce excellent results.

Our Shareholders

We recognize that it is a privilege to have access to the financial resources of our shareholders, and we accept our responsibility to assure them of competent management in return for their investment. We further believe it is important to encourage our employees to own shares by providing stock option and other employee stock purchase and benefit programs.

It is our obligation to plan for consistent and sustained improvement in earnings per share. We intend to maintain a moderately-leveraged balance sheet by employing a reasonable amount of borrowed capital, and to allocate resources to ensure a competitive return on assets employed and stockholders' equity.

We believe in communicating relevant information in accordance with SEC and other regulatory agencies in a timely, professional manner to present and potential investors. In addition, we pledge to maintain strong accounting controls and conservative accounting principles, and to comply with all regulations so that our actions are properly reflected in the records of the organization.

Our Customers

Our long-term prosperity is based upon our commitment to our customers, and theirs to us. We believe in sharing the Company's growth with our customers and the communities in which we operate, through the continuous improvement of our restaurants, meat-processing and other facilities and by using the latest state-of-the-art techniques in nutrition, food preparation, equipment, and service systems. In addition, we want our customers to know we care about them as evidenced by a friendly and hospitable attitude.

Within each of our business segments, we will develop and sustain a lasting advantage by serving the customer better than our competition. Customer satisfaction is judged critical to our success.

Consistent product quality and good customer service are our primary goals. However, while we strive to maximize customer satisfaction, we must also control costs to ensure that we are price competitive and offer a "value." To this end, we will continually seek to improve productivity

and eliminate wasteful management practices, thereby avoiding unnecessary price increases.

We seek a broad range of customers. We will listen and respond to their needs and desires and seriously consider any ideas or complaints they present. In responding to our customers' needs, each improvement to our concepts or products will be based on research and will only be implemented when proven to be economically sound by meeting planned operating, marketing, and financial objectives.

Our Licensees

Our licensees and their employees are important participants in the development of our restaurant businesses. Ponderosa, Inc. licenses its business concepts only to those who share our philosophy of consistent high-quality execution and service to our customers. Accordingly, licensees hold the same position with our Company-operated business units in the allocation of staff resources for improved performance.

Our licensees are not only a source of capital, human resources, and system expansion, but also serve as a wellspring of creative ideas to enhance our customer appeal and improve our mutual profitability.

Over the years, our licensees have played a vital role in our development. We look to them in the future to continue that role with the view toward building and enhancing our businesses and profitability.

Our Vendors

We recognize that our vendors and others we do business with are an important ingredient in our ongoing success. We seek to build long-term relationships that are mutually satisfactory and which help us achieve the service, quality and price advantages we need for competitive success. In addition, our vendors should provide us with research support and be a source of creative ideas for product improvement.

Our People

Ponderosa recognizes that people of all faiths, ethnic backgrounds and walks of life have made important and lasting contributions to the success of our business. Therefore, we will maintain hiring standards and a working environment which will provide an equal opportunity for all, regardless of age, religion, sex, national origin, handicap or color.

We believe that equal opportunity is more than just a legal obligation. Ponderosa has both a moral and a social obligation to ensure that everyone is given an opportunity to demonstrate his or her abilities and to benefit according to their respective contributions to the Company.

Personal Needs: We know that the people who walk in our doors to work with us each day are more than just employees of Ponderosa, Inc. They are also husbands, wives, mothers, fathers, sons and daughters—one-of-a-kind individuals with complex lives and sometimes, complex needs. And when a personal or work-oriented problem is making life difficult, it is also making job performance difficult. Ponderosa will make an effort to provide care and attention to each employee when needed, to help them accurately assess their problem and find a way to resolve it. However, this effort can only succeed if the employee wants it to.

We do this because we are concerned about each employee's personal well-being, and also because it makes good management sense by minimizing turnover of skilled and talented people.

Development: The success of Ponderosa is dependent on the intelligence, creativity, and commitment of our people. Each person's performance is important. It is our goal to staff all echelons of the Company from within, whenever possible and practical. To this end, we will commit the financial resources necessary to develop our human resources internally.

Human resource development is a long-term, ongoing proposition. It entails building a strong organization through delegation of responsibility, thorough on-the-job training, and formal developmental opportunities and activities.

Development is a two-way street. Company and employees share a dual obligation to maximize the effectiveness of the process. Ponderosa will provide a training environment and a full measure of encouragement and expects employees to respond with equal commitment.

The primary objective of development is not necessarily promotion, but superior job performance and satisfaction. The acquisition and honing of well-rounded general management skills are essential for people who occupy or aspire to positions of leadership. We place a significant value on our managers' ability to lead and to attract, as well as retain and develop profit-motivated, competent people at all levels within their area of responsibility.

Rewards: We believe employee compensation should be based on the employee's performance, fairly measured against well-defined objectives. Because of the scope of our operations, our base compensation must be competitive both nationally and within the local areas in which we operate.

Organization: Ponderosa, Inc. is an organization composed of various strategy centers designed to compete effectively in each of our business segments. Responsibility for performance is delegated to general managers. These managers must be given the authority and latitude to accomplish goals consistent with corporate objectives and policies. We believe this environment will stimulate and develop management expertise.

A competent, professional and responsive corporate staff will be maintained to serve the needs of the Corporation and support the strategy centers.

The Climate At Ponderosa

Ponderosa, Inc. strives for a stimulating and challenging climate which emphasizes the full participation of all employees, with a productive interaction between managers and their people, and a strong professional association among peers.

Freedom to Speak and Act

We believe each employee should be heard. We encourage people at every level to voice their ideas. Good business judgment, concern and caution are useful qualities, but fear of being wrong or second-guessed should not be allowed to inhibit innovative suggestions or actions. We believe Ponderosa people should feel free to take a reasonable chance.

Managers have a special responsibility to ensure that employees' ideas are thoughtfully and sincerely evaluated, that each employee's legitimate concerns and grievances are addressed, and that each receives all rights and benefits of employment as outlined in Company policies.

We seek an environment founded on trust and confidence in which all people within the Company can be open with one another. Such a working relationship between individuals or departments can make a significant and positive impact on the results of our Company.

Recognizing Individual Qualities

We value individuality. We will not try to make everyone fit into the same mold. By allowing people to be themselves, we expect to bring fresh ideas and increased productivity to our business. We will maintain a working environment, both physical and mental, that supports a high level of employee performance and energy.

In this environment, there will still be the basic requirements of discipline and policy adherence in order to maintain consistency and order.

Beyond these basic elements, we expect to create an environment that fosters development of the following human qualities:

- Pride, one of the essential forces that moves us.
- Self-reliance and the ability to handle delegated authority independently.
- Courage to be open with one another and to change our minds as we receive new facts and new insights from each other.
- Self-determination. With the knowledge that people grow at different rates and have varying needs, we will create an attitude of trying to bring out the best in people, giving them the opportunity to shape their own lives and careers.

Achievement

Our standard is excellence, to be the best at what we do. We are dedicated to managing our human and capital resources to achieve this goal.

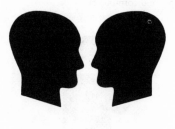

Citizenship

We are committed to fulfilling our basic responsibility to our community and our country by conducting our affairs as good corporate citizens. On a national basis, as well as in other countries in which we operate, we will comply with all duly established laws, ordinances and regulations.

We encourage all employees to become more aware of, and to actively participate in, the governmental process at all levels; to work for the betterment of their communities; and to assume leadership positions with community organizations and causes consistent with their importance to the community and the interests of the Company.

With a strong belief in political and economic freedom, it is appropriate that we devote resources to support the private enterprise system. We recognize a special obligation to those young people whose employment by Ponderosa, Inc. may be their first "real job," by providing a work experience and leadership that fosters a belief in, and support for, the values of the private enterprise system.

Code of Business Conduct

It is our firm belief that integrity is one of the most important characteristics a company can possess. Proper, ethical and legal business conduct with the public and with our employees will enable us to maintain that objective.

Our "Corporate Code of Business Conduct" states the Company's policies, based upon ethical convictions and business experience. Its purpose is to provide guidance to Ponderosa employees which will enable them to avoid situations or actions that could adversely affect the Company's reputation, competitive position, future growth or financial standing. Each employee has the responsibility to become thoroughly familiar with this document and will certify understanding of its contents at the time of employment and each year thereafter.

Our experience indicates that code violations usually arise through misunderstandings. Therefore, managers have the direct responsibility to maintain an awareness of the code and its contents with their employees through open, consistent communications.

Policies in the Code of Business Conduct must be followed without exception.

In Summary

Ponderosa, Inc. is comprised of human, social, operational and financial systems. Its growth, like that of industry in general, evolved with primary emphasis placed on the development and maintenance of operational and financial systems.

In today's society, we think it is important to emphasize equally the social and human systems within our organization. We believe that the final test of our policies, plans and procedures will be determined by the degree to which these systems support and enhance the well-being of our shareholders, customers, licensees, employees, vendors and communities.

Appendix C
Sample Forms

Chronological Data Capture Form

Name_____

Address_____

_____

Telephone_____

Education:

     High School_____

     Location, Date Graduated_____

     College_____

     Location, Date Graduated_____

     Degree_____

     College_____

     Location, Date Graduated_____

     Degree_____

     Other Specialized Education or Training:

_____

_____

_____

_____

_____

_____

_____

_____

_____

_____

_____

_____

_____

_____

Present or Most Recent Position

From_____   Company_____
      (Month)   (Year)   Location_____
To_____   Position_____
      (Month)   (Year)

Responsibilities:_____
_____
_____
_____
_____
_____
_____
_____
_____
_____
_____
_____
_____

Accomplishments:_____
_____
_____
_____
_____
_____
_____
_____
_____
_____
_____

Compensation:_____
_____
_____
_____

From_____   Company_____
      (Month)   (Year)   Location_____
To_____   Position_____
      (Month)   (Year)

Responsibilities:_____
_____
_____
_____
_____
_____
_____
_____
_____
_____
_____
_____

Accomplishments:_____
_____
_____
_____
_____
_____
_____
_____
_____
_____
_____
_____

Compensation:_____
_____
_____
_____

Hobbies and Community Interests:_____

_____

_____

_____

_____

_____

_____

_____

_____

_____

_____

_____

_____

_____

_____

Marital Status:

    Spouse_____

    Children_____

        _____

        _____

Other Pertinent Data:_____

_____

_____

_____

_____

_____

_____

_____

_____

_____

_____

_____

_____

Company: Green Scene Lawn Care, Incorporated

Position: President & Chief Executive Officer

Responses to Duties and Responsibilities of the Position

1. With the assistance of the chief financial officer, define, develop, review and control such internal operating systems as are required to achieve budgetary and financial-planning objectives. This includes not only the ongoing evaluation of agreed upon targets for overall company operations in the areas of sales, net income, equity per share and income per share, but also the continuous review, protection, and enhancement of corporate assets and their utilization to achieve productivity goals and overall improvement.

0   5   10

2. With sales and marketing management, define, develop, and implement plans and programs which, coupled with high-quality products and services, will assure the satisfaction of customers and the preservation, continuity, and expansion of the company's revenue base.

0   5   10

About the Author

Philip R. Matheny has authored numerous articles on the management selection process. He has an extensive business background which encompasses executive and technical recruiting, general management consulting, computers and information sciences, banking, communications and electrical components manufacture.

Before establishing The Matheny Consulting Group in Columbus, Ohio, in 1980, he spent several years with a respected human resources consulting firm in the Chicago area, in executive and technical recruiting. He has recruited exceptionally qualified men and women for a wide variety of upper and middle management positions including general management, financial, manufacturing, sales and marketing, and human resources positions. In addition, he has located and attracted highly qualified computer and telecommunications, mechanical, electrical and electronic, and civil engineers for positions in research and development, manufacturing, and service organizations.

Mr. Matheny's work experience began with IBM Corporation, where he served for fifteen years in various systems, sales, management, and headquarters staff positions. Following his experience with IBM, he was selected to direct the Automated Customer Services Department of Citibank, New York.

Mr. Matheny has also been a management consultant with the Diebold Group (the worldwide consulting firm) and a vice president of GTE Information Systems, Inc., a General Telephone and Electronics, Inc., subsidiary. More recently, he was vice president and a principal stockholder of an electrical products manufacturing company, where he was involved in all aspects of the company management.

Philip R. Matheny is a native of Ohio and a graduate of The Ohio State University, where he majored in business administration and industrial engineering. His hobbies include golf, bicycling, running, sailing, and bonsai. He resides with his wife in Columbus, Ohio.

DATE DUE

FEB 2 1 1992			
2 3			